SUDDEN ADDRESS

BILL BERKSON

SUDDEN ADDRESS
Selected Lectures 1981-2006

CUNEIFORM PRESS/2010

Cover drawing: "Matter," 1969, by Philip Guston. Charcoal on paper.
Collection: Bill Berkson.

Edited by Gregg Biglieri and Kyle Schlesinger.

ISBN: 978-0-9827926-0-5

Distributed by:
Small Press Distribution
1341 Seventh Street
Berkeley, CA 94710-1409
Tel. (800) 869-7553
Fax. (510) 524-0852
www.spdbooks.org

For more information:
Cuneiform Press
www.cuneiformpress.com

ACKNOWLEDGEMENTS

"Poetry and Painting": slide lecture, San Francisco Art Institute, May 1, 1984 and subsequently at Cranbrook Academy of Art; the Arts Museums of Santa Cruz; University of California, Davis; University of California, Berkeley; Jack Kerouac School of Disembodied Poetics, Naropa Institute, Boulder, Colorado. Published in *Zyzzyva*, Fall 1990.

"Travels with Guston": slide lecture, Denver Art Museum, April 22, 1981, and again at the San Francisco Art Institute, May 30, 1984. Published in *Rocky Ledge 8*, June/July 1981.

"Idealism and Conceit (Dante's Book of Thought)": slide lecture, The Poetry Project, St. Marks in the Bowery Church, April 17, 1984; New Langton Arts, November 21, 1985.

"History and Truth": History of Art Department 2002 Commencement Address University of California, Berkeley, May 24, 2002. Published in *The Sienese Shredder #1*, Winter 2006-7.

"Walt Whitman's New Realism": given at "Celebrating Whitman," Université Paris 7eme—Denis Diderot, UFR d'Etudes Anglophones, July 6, 2005. Published in *Floccinancininibibipilification*.

"Frank O'Hara at 30": Poets House, November 28, 2006.

"'The Uneven Phenomenon'—What Did You Expect?": Paul Mellon Lecture, Skowhegan School of Painting and Sculpture, July 21, 2006.

Many thanks to Jan Butterfield, Ray Mondini, Charles Stephanian, Bob Holman, Trevor Winkfield, Brice Brown, Howard Junker, Olivier Brossard, Maureen O'Hara, Karen Koch, Jordan Davis, Ron Padgett, Eric Athenot, Anne Wagner, T.J. Clark, Renny Pritikin, Judy Moran, Anne Waldman, Reed Rye, George Tysh, Diane Vanderlip, James Melchert, Dan Connally, Yvonne Jacquette, Linda Earle, Tracy Horgan, Stephen Motika, Anselm Berrigan, Eric Malone; and, as ever, to Constance Lewallen.

All of these texts were written to be talked, some with slide projections. Most were written, so to speak, on demand: "Poetry and Painting," for instance, I wrote when asked to put together a formal lecture on the subject as a kind of screen test for being hired at the San Francisco Art Institute. "Travels with Guston," on the other hand, served as the prelude to a gallery walk-through of the Guston retrospective then on view at the Denver Art Museum and later formed the second part of my Art Institute audition. (With those and other early talks I discovered the allure of a copy-and-paste method of self-repetition.) Although I had already taught reading and writing courses for some twenty years, I joined the Liberal Arts faculty at the Art Institute in 1984 as a kind of art historian without portfolio and soon found the theatricality of talking in a semi-dark auditorium with slide show accompaniment generally more exciting than the common posture in a literature class or poetry workshop, sitting locked at the end of a table behind a pile of books and papers. Then, too, the pleasures and terrors of standing at a podium to divest myself of whatever putatively was on my mind is something very different from simply getting up and reading my poetry aloud. Such matters aside, after twenty-five years of trying it on, the genre of lecturing, a.k.a. making and delivering a text to be spoken, continues to be enticing. I am grateful to Kyle Schlesinger of Cuneiform Press for suggesting that a selection of such pieces might be possible, and to Kyle and Gregg Biglieri for their care in seeing the project through.

B.B.

CONTENTS

1

Towards the end of her lecture "What Are Masterpieces and Why Are There So Few of Them" Gertrude Stein had this to say:

> I write with my eyes not with my ears or mouth. I hate lecturing because you begin to hear yourself talk, because sooner or later you hear your voice and you do not hear what you say. You just hear what they hear you say. As a matter of fact as a writer I write entirely with my eyes. The words as seen by my eyes are the important words and the ears and the mouth do not count. I said to Picasso, the other day, 'When you were a kid you never looked at things.' He seemed to swallow the things he saw but he never looked, and I said, 'In recent years you have been looking, you see too much, it is a mistake for you.' He said, 'You are quite right.' A writer should write with his eyes and a painter paint with his ears. You should always paint knowledge which you have acquired not by looking but by swallowing. I have always noticed that in portraits of really great writers the mouth is always firmly closed.

Poetry and painting—the "interrelation of the arts" happens because everyone has to take their ideas out for a walk. We enjoy the adaptability of ideas beyond the physical circumstances that may have occasioned them. Who needs ideas, or how important are they in actual practice? It's said that Degas told Mallarmé that he, Degas, had some wonderful ideas for poems, and that Mallarmé let Degas in on a professional secret: "But Degas," said Mallarmé, "poems are made with *words*, not ideas."

Some people suspect that it's mischievous or arcane when two arts, except maybe words and music, cooperate, marry, or intermingle. But poets have loved painting with a vengeance ever since Dante said to Giotto, "How come you make such beautiful paintings—and such ugly kids?" The point is, no form of behavior exists exclusively. Maybe imagemaking is the closest thing to writing. Painting has a skin. Both painting and poetry occupy fictive spaces in the physical world. But then again, it may be because poetry and painting are more incomparable to one another than to the other arts that their affinity is sealed.

Many poets have had jobs helping painters, have sat for them long hours, naked no less, in unnatural poses on lumpy sofas. Poets write about paintings as parts of the world, inhale clouds of turpentine for deeper insight into technicalities, marry the painters male and female, live with whatever favorite works they can scrounge (and pay off divorce settlements with them later)—but that's all only human, it's no cabal.

You can do a lot with educated eyes. What I mean by "educated" is simply how pictures, among other things, can teach you about how to see, and what's visible when you look hard enough or most openly. At a certain point, past the shock of actually seeing, you want to do something about it. That's what makes an artist begin being an artist in the first place. At one time or another you get hit like with a rock. I have a theory that the course of anyone's artistic life is determined largely by the attempt to retrieve that original rock, or what the painters used to call The Dream. Such a prime matter is easy to forget, like dreams. But when you look hard enough or most openly, you are reminded by some sensation like color or light that reflects or refreshes your living space. Just as when you have been glued to a screen, in the street you see people or a slice of sky, and the sensation is continuous. Your ordinary vision is suddenly invigorated or heightened. That sustenance has some staying power. I know I owe some of the presence of my alertness to looking at paintings.

Everyone looks at pictures, and many painters are not dyslexic. Any poet who isn't also a painter or a draughtsman has to admit that there's some envy in the bargain. Gertrude Stein said she was hopeless when it came to trying to draw objects, she saw no relation between the piece of paper and the object she was trying to draw. And that's been exactly my experience too. I doodle, I trace, I fake it, but I can't draw, so to speak, from life. So in looking at and thinking about painting, I have this more or less common vicariousness. It's no sob story. One shouldn't get too entranced by the materialism of art.

Some painters seem baffled by poets because they think poets don't work as hard. Is poetry a residue? Similarly, a poet may fantasize no end about the manual luxury in painting—that no matter how bad you feel or how "nothing," you could just pick a brush, slap some colors around, and given a few skills, arrive at a beginning at least—as opposed to the awesome blank page facing the awesome clogged febrile word-brain. It's nice to dream like that and then get back to base: paint on canvas, words on paper.

There's an "everything" principle—the universal "everything" principle—that poetry and painting share. It has to do with including. Fairfield Porter says, "There is an elementary principle of organization in any art that nothing gets in anything else's way, and everything is at its own limit of possibilities." Any divergence from the "everything" principle is obfuscation, which often is necessary as a ground swell, to add surface. Surface is the great revealer. Both poetry and painting have surface, but with poetry the location of the surface is harder to pin down. With paint, color, the issue of revelation becomes paradoxical. As Robert Smithson reminds us, "The word *color* at its origin means to 'cover' or 'hide'; matter eats up light and covers it with a confusion of color." In poetry, surface may be a matter of complete apprehension of materials across the junctures of word or phrase and interval (or blank). Surface, finally, is what connects the dots. Take this from Schuyler's "The Morning of the Poem":

So many lousy poets
So few good ones
What's the problem?
No innate love of
Words, no sense of
How the thing said
Is in the words, how
The words are themselves
The thing said: love,

Mistake, promise, auto
Crack-up, color, petal,
The color in the petal
Is merely light
And that's refraction:
A word, that's the poem.
A blackish-red nasturtium . . .

In Michael Blackwood's movie of Guston at work, you get to see the beautiful gesture Guston makes as he walks slowly back towards the painting to put on more paint: He's sort of swimming through the air like a Chinese dancer, and the hand not holding the brush is blocking off a certain area of the composition as he zeroes in. It's still a composition at this stage, and on the soundtrack he's saying, "Well, everybody has notions. But notions are not reality. Reality is when you feel to take pink paint and you put it down and for some mysterious reason, some magical way, it becomes a hand—then that's painting. The public, the looker, thinks you have some kind of blueprint for it—there isn't a blueprint . . ."

When Poetry meets Painting, in Padua circa 1306, Giotto and Dante are drinking and gesticulating about the positions of the figures in Giotto's *Last Judgment*. In 1959, when Poetry meets Painting, art is more on the side of the painters but the painters are being generous with it because poetry is less always about having seen paintings and is acting more like itself, more like painting that no one's dreamed of yet.

When Poetry meets Painting, we begin to wonder about Art. It seems poets would never say "Art" without knowing painters, but the painters can't talk about it without knowing poems. Real painters do know poems. To be more specific, I met painting in the spring of 1959 in the form of de Kooning's landscape abstractions at the Janis Gallery in New York. Before that, art meant the Metropolitan Museum near my home where as a child I saw a reconstructed Egyptian tomb and displays of fifteenth-century armor. And color slides of Gorky and Mondrian in college.

In New York, then, the signal gesture was de Kooning's expansiveness and speed, which suggested spatially the kind of surface excitement poetry was beginning to take on as well. A year later, seeing Philip Guston's work—especially his drawings with their slower accumulation of image—I was struck in a different way. The mass-effect of his line was more like a confirmation. In the case of de Kooning I felt, "Oh God, I'd love to write like that," but I'd have to hurry up. I wasn't fluent at that level. Whereas, with Guston I felt "I *do* write like that"—having some inkling of his process, a fellow inchworm!—"and there's something in it too!" Something similar occurred in reading and knowing Frank O'Hara, and loving his incredible acumen, I tried to approach it but couldn't hold on. I had to realize I didn't work that way, attractive as it might seem. My drive was more stubborn, contemplative; and more like Guston, I wasn't so convinced about what the subject matter was. I couldn't say as O'Hara did, "What is happening to me goes into my poems," which implies an instantaneous sweep approaching the speed of light. But I could say, with Guston, "I want to end with something that will baffle me for some time" and "I just want to nail something so that it will stay put."

So the early '60s became an extended invitation for me into the facts and mysteries of hometown New York art. That "splendid state of confusion" was due partly to the residue of heroism, '50s-style, in the air, although by then it was becoming millions-in-business-as-usual. The city was the center of a general cosmopolitan alert that lasted about another ten years. In the early '60s, criticism's idea of the purity of any separate art—poetry, painting, or dance—seemed like a joke just as it does now. (It became a bad joke for a while in between.) One saw how art and social behavior could be seen as extending from one another and talked about in the same terms—what Alex Katz calls "good urban manners" in alignment with "high-style art." The illuminating essay on that score was Edwin Denby's about de Kooning in the '30s:

> Talking to Bill and to Rudy for many years, I found I did not see with a painter's eye. For me the after-image (as Elaine de Kooning has called it) became one of the ways people behave together, that is, a moral image. The beauty Bill's Depression pictures have kept

reminds me of the beauty that instinctive behavior in a complex situation can have—mutual actions one has noticed that do not make one ashamed of one's self, or others, or of one's surroundings either. I am assuming that one knows what it is to be ashamed. The joke of art in this sense is a magnanimity more steady than one notices in everyday life, and no better justified . . .

It was Edwin too, along with a few other poets, who was quickest to understand exactly what the younger artists were up to—the ones who were emerging or had just emerged. Here is one of Edwin's sonnets from that time:

> Alex Katz paints his north window
> A bed and across the street, glare
> City day that I within know
> Like wide as high as near as far
> New York School friends, you paint glory
> Itself crowding closer further
> Lose your marbles making it
> What's in a name—it regathers
> From within, a painting's silence
> Resplendent, the silent roommate
> Watch him, not a pet, long listen
> Before glory, the stone heartbeat
> When he's painted himself out of it
> De Kooning says his picture's finished

I hope the main connection is becoming clearer. How one can speak, for example, of such a poem as having a scale, beyond the compactness of fourteen short lines, similar to the live aspect of size in painting.

How painters react to poems is fascinating. At one point, in the '70s, I could say that Philip Guston had become a kind of Ideal Reader for my poems, because, lettering and then drawing around some of them—I don't actually know which he did first—he opened up certain poems for me, as to subject. One drawing he made in 1973 incorporates a poem called "Negative," which is about an encounter with a large glass door. As Guston said, "Poems and drawings give each other new powers—energies."

I've lived in California for twenty years—a long time—and oddly enough, there still aren't many California artists that I care about as much as the ones I keep leaving behind. There are some obvious exceptions: California artists whose work I've written about from time to time. But if my eyes have been codified somewhat and not adjusted, I don't think it's a matter of prejudice. Jane Freilicher came from New York to teach for a few weeks in Santa Barbara. She said that getting her first glimpse of the landscape out here she realized what the indigenous painters were up against, if they wanted to confront the values of traditional painting: "that awful palette!" Al Held told me he spent weeks looking out the window of a grand studio on Telegraph Hill and finally made a deal with a printer's collective in the basement: "I spent the rest of my time there painting in a corner with a bare light bulb." It happens that I am married to a painter who grew up in California, Lynn O'Hare. Lynn's paintings are not so much about local color as about how objects can command your point of view or how when light and vision are occluded, the obstructed view proffers a new object of attention. Here's a poem I wrote excited by one of her paintings that had a trellis of flowers in it:

DON'T KNOCK IT
for Lynn

Over piled leaves by the cement porch
trimmed & shook from a blue rug: Hair.
The tangle upwind where it fell from,
where closer a branch makes a hard decision, shock-
definitive. Painting's trellis tide
stemless seamless splurge & spray of
openhanded blue, pink top
constant heart's labyrinthine shuttle.
Can't resist the way it floods, revvying one up
for air: "The flowers are coming!"
A New Yorker's sense of distance: Elbow-edged

you take up a Brussels sprout & peel it.
The right white gates span receptive
to your jubilant rush.

Some painters just delight you. Some confirm your eyes for the everyday. Others actually provoke a subject matter or conception that resurfaces in poems. Some can affect your aspirations like the deepest thought or a sunrise. A painting and a chance remark—both by Alex Katz—got me started on this poem "Baby's Awake Now":

BABY'S AWAKE NOW

And now there is the lively sound
Of a panel truck heading due southwest
Along Elm Road, edge of dusk—
The densest light to see to drive by.

The underbrush has brown fringe
And small silent birds.

I saw the rainbow fire
I saw the need to talk.
I saw a unicorn and a red pony.
And I didn't want any deviled eggs.
I drove home with my collar up.

We're alive. You do alarm me to the fact.
The light is on the window in the air,
And breath comes faster than the hounds
To sanction what remembered, what stuck.

Writing art criticism is less interesting but obviously it's pertinent. It's very demanding. I've written art criticism for thirty years off and on, but never as consistently as some other poets like John Ashbery or Peter Schjeldahl. It's hard to stay fluent with criticism and even harder to keep from getting apathetic about it. Its provisionality is both enticing and maddening. There's the problem that it hardly ever comes clean as either observation or writing; like most journalism—and that's what most art writing is—it doesn't hold up over time.

What's the good of art criticism and why does anyone do it, not to mention who reads it? For one thing, art criticism is a job that pays fairly well, particularly if you do a lot of it. Poets hardly ever get paid for doing what they do best, so they take, usually, the odd jobs they can get and bear. Aside from economic considerations, criticism is a public opportunity to be articulate about something that most people ordinarily let slip away into tangential mutterings: your supposedly silent, non-verbal, on-site responses to works of art. I think of it doubly as commercial expository prose and/or (as Carter Ratcliff once remarked) "language somewhere in the vicinity of what it's talking about." What makes poets' criticism valuable, I think, is that they are interested in these situations of looking not as frames of judgment but as observation for observation's sake: they write to find out what can be said in relation to what they see and hopefully to be communicative of some common pleasure in seeing. Can you say what you see? Can it be described? Or is the feeling of two-way recognition between the looker and the work more interesting to tell about? Pleasure in writing criticism is often connected with the surprise of vernacular—the words that sensibly spring to mind when the mind's eye is on a sizable patch of orange paint seen some hours or days previous. Poets are less interested in evaluation and motive. They know that the best one can hope for is the equivalent vitality of a parallel text, and to that they bring a technical proficiency as befits the job.

Art criticism presumably knows what it's talking about. It has a referent and a topic, more determinately than most poems. The words go across the topic making discriminations. In writing art criticism, I like to put my perceptions, via an occasional headlong (or packed-in) verbal construct, out on a limb. If the limb breaks, I tend to hit the factual aspects of the work under discussion with a thud; if I land on my feet, I can bounce back into—or usefully out of—my tree.

Most criticism makes me mad. Most critics are Philistines in the sense that they ignore the cardinal rule of art practice, which is never to give the game away: under the pretext of seriousness or just by coming on excessively shrewd, they either divulge the mystery or insist there is no mystery. It is important to protect the mystery. Professional manners in criticism involve not giving the game away, respecting the secret of the art's manifold dialectic, and at the same time, knowing when to divulge the obvious.

One gives poetry readings, but the art criticism reading, so far as I know, hasn't happened yet. I'll give it a whirl. This is a paragraph from an article I wrote about Franz Kline about three years ago, which I like well enough, mainly because it stays so specific to my way of looking:

Kline simplified but allowed plenty of noise. His hard finishes show a permeability to vision like the night air. His directional lines make for dual sensations of passage and grip. (Some mid-'50s pictures show similarities in scale between impasto textures and the coarse grain of heavy linen fabric, which account for the palpable tractions). A black-and-white surface gathers sharply and wells towards the observer; moored to the edges it nudges them to expand. The blacks connect to edges or to other blacks, while the whites divide and scintillate. Black and white together or separately careen edge to edge as prodigiously stretched lines. There are things white does that black will never do, and the other way round, like consonants and vowels. Two blacks in the same stretch are distinct and make a difference—not a third color but a shade. In *Lehigh V Span* a long, tapering black plows through a traffic of tones (including shimmers of green, pink, blue), as different whites press forward, projecting more and less solidly than a wall. Given the scale, it's peculiar how close you can look and still see a unified image. The light, as Adrian Stokes said of Turner's light, 'takes actuality to itself.' Among the sheared contours, there's a quasi mathematics—lateral divisions into threes and fives—as in the parts of a sonnet. (There are rhymes as well, like blank / yank / flank / plank.) The light spreads the same way the paint is smeared, though with an extra elasticity. Motion is concretized, a characterization, not an issue of performance, not the painter's gesture as such. It's the picture, not the man who made it, that seems to say with Godard, 'I want to do things, not just name them.'

One of Frank O'Hara's poems begins with the line "Picasso made me tough and quick and the world." There is a sense in his poems of inheriting modernity—and modern art in particular—as an expanded ethos. In the wake of that modernity—in what is now called "postmodern"—we're left with a glacial moraine of endless options—terrible, monstrous, great, and so on. It certainly now seems less a century than a field. Since modern art gave us "everything"—i.e., all the existing forms are here—naturally no one feels that those given forms are enough. The poem-paintings of the '50s and '60s reinforced a ground-zero common sense for poets and painters alike. Now poet-painter collaborations seem to be a lost art, perhaps simply because the day-to-day relations have become more scattered.

Wonderfully, there is no logic why poetry and painting should meet at all. It is not poetry dressing up to be "like" painting, or painting being pro- or anti-literary. Those comparisons are really speechless. I sometimes feel called upon to write a whole other lecture entitled "Why I Am Not a Painterly Poet." The real connections lie elsewhere, with materials which criticism is ever hard put to recognize, because criticism most often doesn't, as art will, talk about everything at once.

San Francisco Art Institute, 1984

2

Travel broadens. I like to go see paintings, but from where I live, except for the paintings in our house, I usually have to travel some distance to see what I want to see, or to be surprised by what I hadn't known about beforehand. To see the Guston show here, and not having seen it in familiar places like San Francisco or New York or even Washington where I almost went to see it last spring, seems kind of odd. I don't mean to say "Denver, of all places!"—but allow for the fact that I am less prepared to know what I've come to look at. Which is good in a way: why should I know, on the basis of memory, anything about these paintings?

I feel a bit as if Philip is calling on me to travel, so to speak, "the length and the breadth of the land" to resume our talks and correspondence. Just as in a letter he once wrote, "Why don't you get *ArtNews* to back a flight here & we could get it all together?" Personally, we didn't see each other all that much. Except for the briefest time in New York, we lived in different towns. We wrote a lot of letters. We collaborated on a book of poems and drawings, and I would have certain pictures of his in mind when writing poems. In December I did fly to New York to join in a poets' homage to Philip's memory.

I always have Clark Coolidge to remind me that the best thing a writer can do in the way of criticism is "continue the dialog." That's the theory of the Parallel Text, where the truest response to a painting or poem is another poem and not an accumulation of idea and description. I subscribe to that theory. For one thing, it keeps you out of the pulpit where the morals of art seem more attractive than engaging it head-on or doing the job. For another thing, once you've honestly looked enough at something, you do sort of figure out everybody else has seen it that way too. I do. Everybody agrees on what it is, so the question now becomes, what are you going to do about it? For weeks now I've been swimming in the Guston Ocean—but of whose devising? Clark was saying frankly there's a point at which we have too many ideas. But the assignment here is: Talk. I'm going to lay out the ideas that persist, so that, hopefully, we'll be spared a lot of congestion.

IF THIS BE NOT I / THE STUDIO

"If this be not I—then what?" There are no "three careers." Guston didn't switch styles, there isn't that much style to go around. Guston's touch, the way the paint goes across the canvas, his light, and imaginary space are so consistently recognizable, you sometimes forget to even notice them. The touch is so smooth and gentle and matter-of-fact. It's not like handwriting with a flourish. The eeriness of his images is contained by it, the way horror and absurdity are contained—I mean, held together—by Kafka's plain statement of event. Not a wasted motion in this painting. It's all twos and threes. It's a near square with a bunch of other forms in it. It's a painter doing three things at once. The smoke hasn't settled, and that can has the most exact weight. Why is the brush-hand red? Why is the sky blue? Is that black thing a door?

There's an "everything" principle—the universal "everything" principle—that painting and poetry share, more than the other arts, though you might find it in dancing too. And it has to do with including. I'll explain it later. Any divergence from the "everything" principle is obfuscation, often as necessary as a groundswell, to add surface. But surface is the great revealer. "Art invites recognition of more than it ostensibly shows." Think of all the beautiful obfuscation we've seen since at least the fourteenth-century. With paint, color, this issue becomes paradoxical: "The word 'color' means at its origin to 'cover' or 'hide.' Matter eats up light and covers it with a confusion of color."

At that level, style is overrated, it's less interesting than the wheelbarrow from which stuff is thrown. In Michael Blackwood's movie of Guston at work, you get to see the beautiful gesture Guston makes as he walks slowly back towards the painting to put on more paint: He's sort of swimming through the air like a Chinese dancer, and the hand not holding the brush is blocking off a certain area of the composition as he zeroes in. It's still a composition at this stage, and on the soundtrack he's saying, "Well, everybody has notions. But notions are not reality. Reality is when you feel to take pink paint and you put it down and for some mysterious reason, some magical way, it becomes a hand—then that's painting. The public, the looker, thinks you have some kind of blueprint for it—there isn't a blueprint . . ."

ATTAR

This painting has been famous for its beauty for so long. And you know how that can sort of put things out to pasture. It's the *lyric* Guston, right? Lyric, then Dramatic, and last comes Myth. The Three Ages of the Artist as proposed by James Joyce when he was thinking about Flaubert or Homer. I don't know if that's helpful. I think it actually confused James Joyce plenty later on. This painting is like a rock face, but it's also like a fabulous garden to sit beside. The gardener didn't have a formal plan, no plan, but it didn't just grow there overnight. "A man standing with paint in hand before an empty wall." The ground is given. He steps up to it, so locomotion takes place on at least two planes. Any horizontal mark makes more ground. Any vertical suggests further standing presence or edge. All those suggestions are nothing against the fact that put-on oil paint exists in a fractional space more ours than the wall's. It's a step forward, *towards* but not enveloping. That's why Guston has nothing to do with Monet, but maybe more to do with Turner. But he preferred to speak of Piero della Francesca and Rembrandt, for the exact orientation of their grounds, where their big feelings are declared, not dickered with. A fascinating book by Samuel Edgerton demonstrates that we can only guess how the sweet new science of perspective could have led to what Piero makes manifest, what Guston calls "a necessary and generous law," not linear at all. Everything is standing stock-still in the freeze-frame, but "we can move everywhere as in life."

THE MIRROR

This is called "tonal painting," where there are complements, a lot of agreements, between the colors. No browns. (Maybe just a hint.) Subtleties, nuance, and somewhat stretched relationships spread out in space. You look in the mirror and what do you see? Red, black, green, white, blue, pink, orange, and grey. The paint is put on—*put* is the best word—rather than dragged or splattered or laid-in. This is Guston's dramatic period, much less introspective, no more void. The plot is taking on character. Do we remember what it was like living on earth—picking something up and putting it somewhere? Like your foot, my foot?

SHOE (CELLAR)

The whole progress is so explicit really. You have those crazy shoes that have been everywhere else, clomping around. Now they've arrived sole-first, here. "How long are you going to be in town?" "An object painted on a store window—a shoe—a book—to be seen instantly from a distance." "A sense that I am painting in reverse. I continue the mistake. In the end there is the image I have been wanting to see." "You're painting a shoe; you start painting the sole, and it turns on the pavement (in your head), flattens out slightly (in a more conversational space), and rolls with its dark side turned out flat into a flat land of plaster cast by shadows." "I just want to nail something down so it will stay still for awhile." "You can't peel it off." "Doubt itself becomes a form." "The mirror living which art is." "When the emotion runs out."

PAINTING, SMOKING, EATING

Guston, related by Coolidge: "What's wrong with feeling bad?" William Carlos Williams, related to Guston: "WORK—when up, drive in—When down, assume the clerk—There's plenty of time for both. Work *all* the time. Manic depression, yes, but learn to use yourself."

I asked my wife if the *stillness* in Guston's paintings bothered her. She said: "All those things are painful to him. He paints his fears. That table saw's going to cut those guys up. He's a slice-of-life painter. But no, those little paintings don't have those fears—the cup, the chair, the book—they're fearless. I love his line. Perfect. Not automatic at all . . ."

There are about ten of Philip's pictures in our home, but I'm going to deal with only half of them. And the slides aren't them, but more or less equivalent. First, a drawing I picked out of his studio in 1962, one of those non-stop weaving ones with many loose ends. The lines tend to cross, and there's a lot of air, like drawing in air. Near the top is a circle, ambiguous about being either a balloon or a rock. In the middle, another funny shape, squared-off at one end and narrow like a cardboard box for long thin charcoal but tapered-off at the other end like a syringe. Then at the bottom is a kind of schlong like the tracing of an actual thumb pressed flat. Can you see it? This drawing has all the doubting kind of energy I admired from the start—in Guston's drawings especially—the clean exposure of feeling that unsure, of willing it not to be knee-jerk or banal, short-circuiting that, but being able to trace the discovery of feeling, moving every necessary way with it.

PAW

The next drawing is the converse, more a sure thing, communicated to me by Guston when he sent it as one of the drawings for *Enigma Variations*. The poem it was to go with has conditional aspects—I mean, it starts out as direct-address apology and then proceeds to counterattack. There's a skirmish and then the combatants just stop and look over the side of the road—because they're really just driving home on a mountain.

> Like angels, I can only arrive
> On the point of your admiration,
> And what kind of thing is that
> For a grown man?
>   But what I really want
> Is to do what I can
> For nothing in particular,
> Letting the black holes rip,
> As they may, through your lives,
> And golden light on the stones
> Just before sundown, anywhere.

"Anywhere" means home. So Philip said, OK, true as far as you go, but, given all that, this is where you really come to roost, like Gertrude Stein saying that writing is not about Identity at all, but the Beast Hand of the artist and his line. I wish I had the words for it but can't find the letter he wrote, which was about remembering one's obsessive vocation. An interesting sidelight about the line "What kind of thing is that / For a grown man?" is that it comes from a conversation years before the poem with another painter about—should I spill the beans here?—a composer's work, which seemed all too minimalist (no beans) for him. So the painter—it was Alex Katz, naturally enough—said "What kind of thing is that for a grown man to be doing?!" And I thought that was the most sublime form of criticism ever! What a thing to say. It never occurred to me until then to think of artists as grown-ups at all.

CUP

Next is the primary lesson of four little paintings he sent just before our son Moses was born. Reading from top to bottom: An open blank book, a personal mailbox with a brick on top, a red/black cup, absolutely monumental against levels of grey/black/green, and a big easy chair with studs, flat, dirty white edged with black. "Dear Bill, As I was mounting these little oils, I thought how nice they would look hung on your wall as a cluster, joining the small one you have of a canvas on an easel. They look to me like a primary lesson—The Book, The Chair, The Cup, and of course The Mailbox—also as a little present to you and Lynn and baby. Soon, no? Naturally, the book is for baby—not a mark on it—yet—clean. All you will need is a hammer (I mean, to hang them on the wall)."

BLACK SEA

What is the world of these later paintings like? What's it feel like to live there, with all the prepositions of time involved, like something on the table. It's unusual for anybody, artists included, to deal with the whole world and not some convenient corner of it. In the corners, being manageable, being what most daily life affords, some very wonderful things can happen. As Williams says, "You can do lots if you know what's around you." So we don't knock still life or portraiture or just a beautiful sense of color that reflects or refreshes our living space. That sharpens our eyes. But Guston seems to be reflecting on the most complete earthly physics. That's his scale, whatever circumstances haunted him to get there. He said he didn't even like William Carlos Williams, he liked T.S. Eliot. Be that as it may, I find that looking at a Guston and then turning to some flowers in the room or a piece of wall or street, my sight is invigorated and heightened, just as when I've looked at a Williams poem or a painting by Vermeer.

And these earthly physics don't sidestep the seriousness of human relations—from say, monolog to marriage to public address, on out. They include consciousness of the horror—of cruelty, of evil, of preposterous shitty politics. The size should inform you that they're public images, not the mutterings of any guy in a room, not rhetoric either. I would have liked to have heard Guston talk about the videotape of the shooting of Ronald Reagan in Washington. If you're going to talk about that, other than to just say "ouch" or "How ghastly!" it's got to be in terms of what you saw, as a witness. It's as if Godard's movies had predicted the space of it. Or, as in Guston, it's focused by the band of street and the edges of it, cement sidewalk and brick wall. And then the explosive group positions. The group with Reagan in it, drawing tight, the shift of his one eye, at the shots. The instant huddled enclosure, and *masking*, of the gunman by other gunmen. The suddenly faceless weights of Brady and the Secret Service guy on the sidewalk. Brady facedown. The shots in the slow-motion playback like footfalls in a tunnel, the way these men get shoved to their sanctuaries, the cars—you can imagine the soles of their shoes turning over . . . This is exactly the world Guston is dealing with, and it's just like home. Could it be gravity that makes everything so ceremonious around here? "I feel as if I have been living with the Klan." You don't need a lot of features to have a face.

WHEEL

A couple of years ago, while living just outside New York, I went into town expressly to see two shows that were there at the same time: November 1979 to be exact, Guston and de Kooning, with about ten blocks of midtown New York meditation-space between them. They meditated on each other beautifully. The Gustons had that fixated look—not rigid, "unsettled" like he says—but perfectly structured like a sentence that stops you in your tracks. At the opening Rudy Burckhardt said, "They're so funny, I didn't know he was so funny." The de Koonings were more of a roller-coaster ride. They had natural movement, only speeded-up, like a windstorm or an earthquake. With Guston, every painting guides you to a place where its particular image can be delivered whole. If you move around, it stays the same image, imperturbable. In de Kooning, you get more caught up in *his* space, in the shift of focus, multiple, slippery, headlong, always coming at you with more. What de Kooning and Guston share, I think, is a degree, not exactly a quality of light—generous to, not interrupted by, detail. Such observations make looking at these pictures sound reasonable. But Guston's a raving enigma. De Kooning's a raging bull.

PYRAMID AND SHOE

The next spring New York had the magnificent big Picasso show. There were so many unsuspected pictures, and so little about history or period charm. I was surprised that, aside from theory (which was no help), I didn't know how to look at the earliest high Cubist works at all, not until they had letters in them. And the full-blooded finale, the late works, was shocking, terrific, it rocked every premise of the Museum of Modern Art as such. The whole show certainly wasn't arguing the benefits of modern sensibility. It dispelled the notion of "modern" and "postmodern" right along with it. Instinct is not modern, and in Picasso the nature of art is unalloyed instinct for about ninety years. Maybe it doesn't matter how soon, or how long it takes to come home to it. But Guston, running his own course over fifty years, shows it's possible for instinct of that nature to emerge with a lot of conscious sweat and to be sustained in the midst of every stupidity and collapse our time has to offer. In fact, he made the question of that instinct the subject matter of his work.

Homestretch: The New York School, which term Guston liked better than abstract expressionism, has only one unifying principle really— aside from the "New York" part of it—and that is Surface: Respect for the whole inexhaustible but truly personally limited surface of what's at hand—somebody is making a painting or writing a poem. It's not like God speaking, although you don't necessarily rule that out either. Respect for surface is so traditional that you can antagonize every other aspect of what's been handed you, but more to put in than to leave out whatever seems life-like at the time. Fairfield Porter says the great realization of the painters in the '50s was of a closure in the life-likeness of subject and object where everything, the entire set, inside and out, became material to the work. As Frank O'Hara would say, "You just jump in and deal with it." If you have a plan or some rules, a model coming at 5 or a fixed vocabulary you feel like arranging, they'd be as contingent as that day's air or your thoughts about destiny. In Guston, the simultaneous pressurings of composition and final image re-realize this principle as part of the painting's life as fact. "You can't peel it off." You can't dispose of it either.

None of this is restful, I guess, and there's still too much pith. You can ponder these Gustons, or you can recognize how true, see the humor, and let them pass. But not dispose of. Curiosity isn't really ponderous. The pictures are not the kind to let your mind go off on tangents. They really want you to stay and talk. They speechify. An old bean floats on the table of the sea. Somebody tossed the moon up there. The book is blank, all yours, fill it. Maybe someday you'll grow powerful enough to shake that cup. But who wants to?

> We are in great spirits these days—I've gotten to love my secluded way of living—painting at all hours, reading a lot (History-Pre-History)—I don't know why—it just hit me—and I'm *fascinated*. Early man, the first art—language and so on. Right now it connects with thoughts and images I'm involved with. Feel good to be 'outside' of the present. Maybe it's the only way to see and feel the present. Anyway, many, many new large pictures getting more 'unearthly' and of course this pulls and attracts . . .

The images that appear somehow reveal more in terms of forces than what the images represent. Is it possible? So this is what I've been after—after so many years—a good heavy foot in the door of this room, finally. What a difference—to *live* out a painting—instead of just painting it . . .

Another time, standing in his studio at Woodstock, he looked thoughtful. "Sometimes all you remember from an event is the look in one eye."

Denver Art Museum, 1981

Most of the quotations in the above text are self-evidently from Philip Guston; others are from Larry Fagin, Adrian Stokes, Lynn O'Hare, Robert Smithson and Clark Coolidge.

Dante's book of thought is called *Convivio*, or *Il Convito*, literally a dinner/banquet or manner of entertaining guests. Incredibly, the only translation into English that I'm aware of, Wicksteed's rather archaic one, is out of print. In John Thorpe's copy, from which I'm citing (Temple Classics, 1903), the endpaper indicates the probable date of composition as 1308, when Dante, seven years into exile from Florence, would have been 43. His hindsight on *La Vita Nuova* is that it was adolescent dream, completed on the threshold of manhood. The proposal of *Convivio* is grown-up thought, contemplation, a looking into matters, as well as a new book of poems. In modern Italian, which Dante helped to invent, *convivere* means to cohabit; *convivenza* is life in common; *l'umane convivenza*, human society. Dante is writing from life, allowing for transformations, which cover or multiply the story. The poems form steps of a narrative; if they seem dogmatic, the dogma changes step by step. The first book, *La Vita Nuova*, can be read as a manual on how a young poet enters into poetry. He builds a neighborhood of it and gives it characters, but he never pretends to be in complete charge. In fact, some of his designs have been seriously misconstrued by his peer group. Beatrice, as ever, is a big help, but in *Convivio* she is absent in heaven, or in the wings, or substituted for—absolutely all of the above. I think the Lady Philosophy is another aspect of the same person, the person of Dante's impulse toward poetry and exaltation.

Convivio builds upon the rumors of wrong turns. It's also a process of retrenching Dante's poetry self in the neighborhood of the original impulse: it got away from him, bounced off, he fell into troubled dreams, had doubts. Demanding circumstances woke him up. The compassionate lady in the window, leaning on the sill, distracts him from his sense of loss; a possible infidelity, he admits as much. She is also the rock lady, heart of stone. To know her is to be prepared for "anguished sighs." But as *Convivio* progresses, she is revealed as the genuine guiding substance of his restorative thought.

Dante is pulling together a huge nebula of thought forms and aligning them with the elements of his experience. He writes of "adjusting the sail of reason to the breeze of his desire." As a dutiful commentary on his recent work—fourteen odes, of which only three are actually treated— the project is logically incomplete. Wicksteed in his commentary was shortsighted, I think, in claiming that "the dominating motive . . . was a passion for study and promulgation of philosophic truth." Dante's citations of the thinkers barely disguise his glee at seeing through and confounding their arguments, their "dear, gorgeous nonsense." You see how sharp Dante could be, how subtle his amusement. Not to slight the philosophers though: he spins their constructs 360 degrees, but he couldn't begin to work out their original systems. The three odes he comments on aren't what he says about the meanings of them either. They are even less moved by his rationales than the sonnets in *Vita Nuova*. But the overlay effect is enlarging.

Osip Mandelstam says about Dante's vernacular: "Here everything is turned inside-out; substance is the goal, and not the subject of the sentence." *Convivio* is fine-tuning. In the *Comedy*, which is vision, and especially in the cantos of the *Inferno*, there's this slapstick element. Without the expert guidance of Virgil (admittedly, we don't know if Virgil ever did this before either!), without Virgil to look to and ask, Dante would lose his footing, take pratfalls, turn the wrong way into oncoming traffic. As it is, he is subject to fainting spells. Dante's work is basically about gravity anyway, including passages of light. Almost every scene in the inferno threatens to turn either clownish or disastrous. If you cast it as a movie, the obvious choice to play the lead would be Buster Keaton. Buster plays Dante. They're lookalikes too. Dante portraits are always tightlipped, same bony nose, pronounced cheekbones, bruxism. Generous expanse of eyelid over hard, fixed pupil . . . Mandelstam sees an interesting parallel in Dante's native tongue. He says:

When I began to study Italian and had only just become slightly acquainted with its phonetics and prosody I suddenly understood that the center of gravity . . . had been shifted closer to the lips, to the external mouth. The tip of the tongue suddenly acquired a place of honor. The sound rushed toward the canal lock of the teeth. Another observation that struck me was the infantile quality of Italian phonetics, its beautiful childlike quality, its closeness to infant babbling, a sort of immemorial Dadaism.

CHE FA?

All of Dante's work reads as a perpetual induction ceremony. For a poet, that seems to be consistent with the facts of practice. As community exists, Cavalcanti's heartfelt reply to Dante's early sonnet is the first positive charge, and Guido is then and there Dante's first/best friend. In the meadow of Limbo, "on the enameled green," on the outskirts of Hell, Dante sees Virgil regroup with the four great shades of classic poets, so that they make a circle of five:

> Thus I saw assembled the fair school of that lord of highest song who, like an eagle, soars above the rest. After they had talked awhile together, they turned to me with sign of salutation, at which my master smiled; and far more honor still they showed me, for they made me one of their company, so that I was sixth amid so much wisdom. Thus we went onward to the light, talking of things it is well to pass in silence, even as it was well to speak of them there.

In Dante's number scheme, six leaves room for a seventh, or 7-8-9 (three more), or multiples thereof. This is good news. Dante is not being preemptive. In *Convivio*, he announces his ambition to achieve a certain level of nobility in his work, "not that I am a good worker, but that I aspire after such." Only in Limbo, it seems, can there be any sense of "home-free-home."

Everything's caked but "human" and "art" aren't "thing" and "that." You may stare politely, however reintroduced. All Dante's work is stations, which makes it complete, one poet's mass transit. So what I want to

37

talk about is the idealism implied in moving transit that figures as an impulse reoccurring at a series of stations. (It might be the flashes at I-beams as the express grinds through.) This presentation is meant as entrance to the topic with banged-together quotations; a roughing-out, a spillway, a pounce, a show and tell with pictures as points of refraction as if we were speaking at your house/my house with concomitant "wild surmise." The topic, I feel, is tricky. There's no hierarchy or exclusivity implied, but I will conjure up only my own examples.

Talking on the phone with Ted Berrigan three years ago, it occurred to both of us more or less simultaneously that when poetry meets painting, when we as poets met painting, we begin to know about Art. Probably any artist begins making art from what feels to him like an intensely subjective state. Whatever got him to perform such an act, including whatever experience he may have had with already existing art, probably feels to him completely oddball, even aberrant, from his own social point of view. The risks in that respect are real but the dangers are outweighed by the pressure of an instinct, or whatever force issues the command to proceed. The feeling that there's something right that won't be put off. Therein lie the ideal conditions for the first real work, even though that work may be disowned later on, under conditions known loosely as "maturity." Art comes from art, so the story goes—and true, but in America and perhaps elsewhere, a lot of art burgeons forth in a terrific confusion of standards that for a while anyway, and usefully, cancel out. Artists like Philip Guston and Joe Brainard and David Smith began as teenagers to make drawings modeled on the salient artists of *their* worlds—the wonderful cartoonists like Windsor McKay, Herriman, Ernie Bushmiller. Anyone's campfire sense of narrative begins "It was a dark and stormy night."

Probably any artist tends to be interested in how other artists' artistic lifetimes began. The second third, the middle hundred-or-so pages, of an artist's biography, when that's written down, is usually thrilling. As for the rest, childhood is mostly either fraught with phantoms, deprived, or idyllic, a delay unless the parents themselves are interesting. The third third, the grown-up remainder goes along quite predictably as taking-care-of-business, unless there is an emergency. You turn back for curiosity to the work.

In terms of ideals and *un*predictability, a passage by William Carlos Williams in the prologue to his *Kora in Hell* retains its fascination. Williams, anyway, is the exceptional kind of artist about whom you want to know everything. He tells you everything and then you want to know everything else. Frank O'Hara is like that too. In this passage, Williams is discussing, like Shakespeare in the *Sonnets*, art and marriage, and art *as* marriage, and the art of marriage, and he begins on a very funny note:

> I have discovered that the thrill of first love passes! It even becomes the backbone of a sordid sort of religion if not assisted in passing. I knew a man who kept a candle burning before a girl's portrait day and night for a year—then jilted her, pawned her off on a friend. I have been reasonably frank about my erotics with my wife. I have never or seldom said, my dear I love you, when I would rather say: My dear, I wish you were in Tierra del Fuego. I have discovered by scrupulous attention to this detail and by certain allied experiments that we can continue from time to time to elaborate relationships quite equal in quality, if not greatly superior, to that surrounding our wedding. In fact, the best we have enjoyed of love together has come after the most thorough destruction or harvesting of that which has gone before. Periods of barrenness have intervened, periods comparable to the prison music in *Fidelio* or to any of Beethoven's pianissimo transition passages. It is at these times our formal relations have teetered on the edge of a debacle to be followed, as our imaginations have permitted, by a new growth of passionate attachment dissimilar to every member to that which has gone before.

What "allied experiments"? Well might you ask. It's not what you expected. Just what did the good Doctor consider "reasonably frank"? Well, wouldn't the contrary instance be a stalemate over who best committed the rules to memory? Marriage definitively thwarted due to some *a priori* iconography averted in poured concrete? Imagism? Williams' earliest poems found their self-reflection in the active principle of love as the main work, continual, pure, and simple.

A few years ago someone proposed an anthology of poets' first poems, which never happened and probably shouldn't. The story of first poems is possibly like the story of first kiss, your first cigarette, first anything, of first fruit, sky, "first dead hand." It was a dark and stormy night. A poem by John Thorpe tells of the approach:

> One night a kid was thinking
> in bed
> about something.
> It hit him like a rock—
> Poetry, poetry, poetry.

That "it" doesn't equal poetry as such. But that rock is fascinating, as a prime factor. It's not the philosopher's stone, or a diamond even: it isn't a Gibraltar-like assurance, nor in any respect evangelical. A message rock. It's maybe closer to what Jimmy Schuyler called "an active stone." The rock hit, bounced off and rolled away in prosodic paradiddle. I see the kid as getting the head-on point of poetry, and that's what struck him. Induction comes later. Maybe not: maybe another solid body enters the atmosphere in its turn and the kid becomes a billionaire selling microchip secrets to Iran. But, for the sake of argument, say the first rock really makes a permanent dent. Poor kid! Instant dementia! The moment is ideal and unforgettable, like the first objective fact. Growing up absurd, *ergo* something to do. But being transient and uncultivated, it appears to remain subjective. My view of process is that as an artist gets deeper into his work he keeps returning to that original rock, or it comes back around, new, like a comet.

Artistic vitality is partly a sporadic re-acquaintance, a reconnoitering of one's original feelings about art, turning them over and seeing what's inside and under them. And partly also getting struck by other facets, the forces of which are equivalent. Those others are the valuable ideals generated by experiencing what you admire most in art. "A stone is nothing but weather excluded from atmosphere and put in functioning space." As practice, it may be a space-bar pause against the gestalt of false starts and above conceit. Restorative. Underneath, and about to be uncovered, may be several unappetizing creepy-crawly things, and, under them, is the ridgeback of an incommensurate monster, a humungous blob. The discrepancies in process are endless; I don't always like them very much.

Maybe the ideals one has away from writing—the ones a step away from what you're going to do anyway—are nothing but reminders, the way inspirational literature, or religious-philosophical writing, reminds you repeatedly of what you somehow already know or have always meant to commit to memory; but ninety percent of it you forgot dropping your notebook to answer the phone. When Jack Spicer was living in New York, he answered a California friend's complaint about the difficulty of keeping writing poems. The friend in his letter whined: "I don't have a vision." Spicer replied: "You've got it ass-backwards. One doesn't have a vision and then write poetry. Just the opposite. One writes poetry and creates a vision. Life *follows* art. Until you learn that, you're going to keep on chasing your own tail." In practice, this seems pretty obvious. But every artist has his outside reminders.

• • •

Dear Lulu in Hollywood. Obviously the only way to come to a considered statement about ideals is jagged. Ridgebacked. I'm away from my desk. How big a bit can discourse carry? I have to keep reminding myself that this is what happens when the process has strayed from actually writing poems. I may have an abnormal belief in material life. The sounds the point makes are click, tick, buzz, hum, plus some spinal wavering. My mind feels like St. Jerome's little terrier; not so well-groomed, I suspect, but at least sparking upright, a kite in the fog. Let's hope this tumbles somewhere between connoisseurship and oratory. Some day in the process a delicate hand from a cloud blowing by delivers this message: "Be true to the dreams of thy youth." A real-life Herman Melville gets the message and tacks its card to his refrigerator with magnet letters verbatim. Everything you believe about space is so Latinate. It's not what you expected, what do you expect? What otherwise can be the big draw about the Sublime other than that there are no mirrors in it? Where field verges on world, world crystallizes to field. I was born *to*, not *with* this. Other poetries suffer from *anorexia nervosa*, not the world's. Somewhere in here is the realist who does the work, who moves, the practitioner, the grown-up professional. As Stevens said about imagination: "It has the strength of reality or none at all." The craft is frail. Rhetoric is a bobbin-tension. Can't we have a simple active thread?

• • •

What Adrian Stokes calls "the separateness of ordered, outer things" can be verified as a sensation available to anyone with a view, or with just some household amenities on the table. Liking how things look when people leave them alone is a microcosm of the point. Even when managed by anti-material Martians the landscape refuses to yield such a permanent wreck. If motif in paint is so plausible, why aren't there more great nature poets? By which I don't mean pastorals. A fine poet—Ted Berrigan—can muster conceit, realism, and a pure use of eyes, and stepping on the line, end up everywhere but mystical:

> "Everything is really golden,"
> Alice, in bed, says. I look, & out the window, see
> Three shades of green: & the sky, not so high,
> So blue & white. "You're right, it really is!"

In Philip Guston's pictures there is a perfected present face of space you don't expect to move. The artist who is most at home in the middle distance tends to take things at face value. About a portrait he had painted Alex Katz remarked: "I couldn't see the face so I painted the make-up." Guston's "I want to end with something that will baffle me for some time." Where baffle is a transforming device that deflects, furthers circulation, heats shot with gleams, "the mirror living which art is." The apparent motto is: "Quit quoting." This lecture might be about Philip Guston. Allow me to be consistent enough at least to keep quoting him.

Guston writes: "Two artists always fascinate me—Piero della Francesca and Rembrandt . . . Piero is the ideal painter; he pursued abstraction, some kind of fantastic, metaphysical, perfect organism. In Rembrandt, the plane of art is removed. It is not a painting, but a real person—a substitute, a golem . . . Certain artists do something and a new emotion is brought into the world; its real meaning lies outside of history and the chains of causality." In asserting these two, seemingly very modern ideals—on and off "the plane of art"—Guston also pinpoints the discrepancy between ideals and something not. This has nothing to do with being good. Or if it does, it's in the sense of Juan Gris, who was notoriously hard on himself, who wrote: "My painting may be 'bad' great painting but in any case it *is* 'great' painting." The discrepancy then, which Guston often talked about, is between ideals and the sometimes frightful appearance of unknown quantities—monstrosities—that seem unadjusted by intentions. If art is necessarily hybrid, it's most completely so at that level. Ideals may arrive reasonably more or less intact. Specifically, nobody expects either the ideal or the substitute, the identifications of which in reality can be interchangeable. The sort of ideal that Guston was identifying in Piero can't be confirmed by rules. Classicism, for instance, which conceited students like to define as rules-oriented as checkers, eludes its connoisseurs. Henri Focillon says, "Classicism is not the result of a conformist attitude. On the contrary, it has been created out of one final, ultimate experiment, the audacity and vitality of which it has never lost . . . Classicism, a brief, perfectly balanced instant of complete possession of forms; not a slow and monotonous application of 'rules,' but a pure, quick delight, like the *acme* of the Greeks, so delicate that the pointer of the scale scarcely trembles . . ." To translate, I would say it's not taste or theory, but belief and sensation. On the subject of the ideal, it's the continuity of sensation I want to go on about.

Maybe it's what specialists term "a display of qualitative information." For a while now I've been fairly obsessed by the evidence of a particular sensation in art—in painting most conspicuously, but I'm willing to bet the literary examples are rife too. The closest observations of such presence are to be found in the writings on art by the English aesthete Adrian Stokes, whom Guston recommended as the best writer on Piero. "Giorgione, Piero, Vermeer, Chardin, Brueghel, and Cézanne," says Stokes, "are the painters who really interest us the most." The fact that he doesn't take them chronologically is significant; the lineage of sensation as you get it in looking at pictures from place to place is not an art-historical one. Anyway, all of the painters Stokes mentions (and the ones I'll mention too) appeared as odd-men-out in their separate times. None of them generated immediate followings or schools.

Technically, Vermeer and Piero look contradictory but in sensation and significance they join. Pictures by each suggest a kind of knowing in the work, and only in the work, manifest as displayed, and this subsumes such partial aspects as technique, subject matter, local customs, style and so on. One attribute they share is an orientation to things and space as completely visibly positive, something you can see as a passing flash in everyday life but which few people believe in constantly enough to pursue as fact.

The Core Faculty of this sensation, as I see it, is Piero, Vermeer, Chardin and Cézanne. The immediate adjuncts are Brueghel and maybe Seurat, and later some peculiar interlopers like Balthus and Morandi. There are contemporaries who participate in the question of continuance. Other great painters—Picasso, Rembrandt, Van Gogh, de Kooning, Mondrian, Johns, Léger, Giorgione, Titian, Chinese painters of the Sung Dynasty—make interesting parallels. These are obviously not all the great painters—the issue of this sensation isn't possibly, "great painting," but a feeling about what is ostensibly right as well as real. There are other real approaches just as there are other ideal facts.

I guess I should also point out that this is not an antiquarian interest. I'm not arguing a review of bygone golden ages in art or inviting you to a nostalgia party with authoritarianism as the *piéce de résistance*. Nor is it "Let's face it, it's a boring century!" The century, in fact, has been mislaid. What we're left with is its field of endless option—terrible, great and so on. Since modern art gave us "everything"—and all the existing forms are here—naturally no one feels that the given forms are enough.

In Vermeer, the point of entrance is precise and realistic: surface, wall, threshold. The approach is immediate and unfussed. No obfuscation. The subject is simple and inexhaustible; the whole image strikes eye and mind instantly in equal measure like a natural light, a reminder that light is substantial, has pressure and weight. The details of paint aren't particularly gorgeous. The conception is within genre but unruled. The ideal conception is that technique means something, is not a test (not hierarchical, as Pound saw it), but an ongoing state of attention like affection that lasts.

Here is Stokes on Piero, culled from various essays:

> In his book on perspective Piero came near to identifying painting with this science. Except in front of his paintings it is difficult to grasp how much emotion, and in particular a sense of explicit order, how much sense of discovery could have been both stimulated and released by the employment of geometric perspective. The transcendental medieval culture was hostile to the apprehension of homogeneous space, as if the medieval Aristotelian concept of the four elements in the terrestrial zone below and of the divine element above, outmoded the easy contacts of normal vision. But stress upon mathematics, both in the case of Alberti and of Piero, by itself explains nothing of their art. Similarly Platonism and neo-Platonism was but a necessary garment, the cover of a nameless joy in things.

· · ·

> What I call purely visual matter is dissociated from noise as well as from silence, from past, present and future. Things stand expressed, exposed, unaltered in the light, in space. Things stand without temporary association; and in any case, few minds seem to be able to disentangle space from time.

> The finality revealed is too great in Piero's pictures for any such world, the finality revealed even when, like Uccello, he represents a battle in progress. The disposition of shapes by means of color and perspective afford a sense of completeness, so that not only is the purely visual aspect of things stressed, but it is enforced to such a degree that happenings, ferment psychological and physical, are

subsumed under formulae of absolute exposure in terms, that is of unalterable positions in space.

(That seems to jell with Guston's "I want to nail something so that it will stay put.")

We have from him the widest vistas and therein the equal simultaneous constancy of things; a stillness that is not archaic, a fullness without boast, a massive self-containment in the very stream of adult life. But he delighted also to show the virtuosity, as it were, of his rooted shapes in his fondness of temporary structures or of any such apparatus to whose related forms he could, like the dying sun on an autumn day, unexpectedly attribute a durable and self-sufficient sense.

• • •

Things have their own light. They seem less lit from the sky.

Stokes's specifying of "adult" is interesting. "Self-containment." The idea of a grown-up art never seems very fashionable; it is notably absent from biographies, which often seem bent on proffering excuses for an artist's never growing-up. As for seeing the work and enjoying it, a discrete, not addled, face-to-faceness seems the last thing an audience might go for. It's not the general idea of fun. But it is the mainly public characteristic of this sensation I'm going on about. The paintings of Vermeer and Piero especially direct the viewer to stand off on his own two feet, neither enveloped nor pulled in by the active surface; not seduced, tricked, bludgeoned, or swept away or any of those things impressive art is supposed to accomplish at the expense of virtual space. That other art is coercive may be OK; it affects its own bio-reliefs. Here, there are no tricks to the focus; the intermediary space is sort of up to you. But "you" are not to be confused with the activity of the picture.

Fact is a commensurate substance, both primary and convoluted. In art, materials tend to assert their own values. Fresco wall painting—*fresco buono*, as they say—thrives upon a literal crystal effect, "a chemical reaction based on the behavior of lime." Water-based pigment paint sets in a wet plaster wall, "calcium hydrate combines slowly with the carbon dioxide, which is always present in the air, to form calcium carbonate, creating a semi-translucent surface into which the pigments are bound." "The plaster dries and re-crystallizes, the pigment particles are locked among the crystals. Thus the colors become an integral part of the wall's surface, to endure as long as it endures." If Piero is obeying any rules, they are only the implications of his materials at their full extent. No other fresco painter has his crispness.

Contrariwise, put-on paint takes up a fractional space more the viewer's than the wall's, especially with moveable panels or stretcher bars. It's a step towards but not obliged to be intimate. The history of oil painting reads as complicated because of the optional degrees of involvement or aggression in that fractional space—I don't mean just how juicy or muscular the flesh tones, or whether the painter worked with a feather or a trowel. For instance, it may be true that the vicissitudes of the modern New York School painting have hinged on which ways the artists take the space of oil paint, how far, or whether they take it all.

One thing these four painters have in common is how little is known about their personal lives, and how little it seems to matter. The exception is Cézanne, maybe the first painter about whom an entire biographical drama develops almost exclusively from recounting his work habits and thoughts about painting! The most dramatic fact about Vermeer is posthumous: how when he died at 43, leaving his wife Catherine with a writ of bankruptcy and eight kids to feed, Catherine tried almost everything to avoid selling Jan's most sought-after work, *The Painter in his Studio*.

Piero della Francesca appeared as a painter some time in his early 20s. He wrote three important treatises—on perspective, solid bodies in space, and on pure math—the last of which was completed after he stopped painting due to blindness in his late 60s. When he died, around the age of 80, the bookkeepers ranked him as a famous painter in his hometown. Vasari's life of Piero is generously apocryphal, but he described a number of real paintings, which no longer exist. As with

Dante, all of Piero's elements are ones, twos and threes; the work is stations. His actual size is triple. Those eyes are celestially conceived, and they are nuts (walnuts). The lips he depicts are distinctly profane.

Piero's passion for mathematical perspective is seconded by Vermeer's for descriptive optics. The inventor of the microscope, Anthony van Leeuwenhoek, was the executor of Vermeer's estate. (Apparently, he and Catherine didn't hit it off too well—quarrels about the fate of pictures or their values.) Holland was the first big modern nation: it had more glass, more mirrors and windows; the best mapmakers, the center of diamond-cutting, the center of the science of optics—Kepler, Descartes, Spinoza, the Amsterdam Kabbalists, all-around men like Christian Huygens who developed the wave theory of light and invented the pendulum clock. Gerard Dou spent three days painting a broom. Vermeer quite possibly used intricate lens set-ups together with a camera obscura to produce a refraction of the view out his back window onto canvas. The image via the box is dim; the painter puts on the light, the final form, from elsewhere. Direct color painting; no preliminary drawing, no sketches. The surfaces of these pictures in their actual layers are thin. Some of the greens over time suffer an oxidation known as "blue-green disease." The women are local. His daughters may have served as captive models. "Dabs, blooms, gleams," they're also bell-shapes, pearls, parts of the furniture, muses of silence, pregnant pauses, opacity, crystal clear. "The same corner of the same room with the same window," he varies the characters, one or two at a time. It's interesting to remember that the intensity of light in Dutch weather changes minute by minute. We don't expect these spaces to change.

Chardin inherited genre from the lesser Dutch masters by way of the brothers Le Nain. He brought the image forward and softened tones to a slightly unearthly warm frontal glow, derived partly from a discretion about not blending colors. Chardin was born and lived all his life in Paris. He dreamed of being a history painter at court; instead, he got still life, children, peaches, self-portraits, and dead ducks. A certain success. Not all his pictures are interesting, neither are all of Vermeer's. Vermeer's colors are a lot stronger. Chardin is a sincere, perfectly able, model French master. Cézanne admired his precision and feeling. In the nineteenth century his work was liberally compared to Vermeer's whose work he could never have seen. Incidentally, the same man, Etienne-Joseph Théophile Thoré, who first argued the preeminence of Vermeer, also rescued Chardin's reputation. Thoré nicknamed Vermeer "the Sphinx of Delft." He was a radical democrat who under the pseudonym of "Will Burger" wrote steamy editorials with lines like: "All history is a perpetual insurrection against the powers that rule the world."

Francis Ponge says apropos Chardin: "If one takes the down-to-earth as a point of departure and neither makes nor wastes any effort trying to rise to an exalted or splendid level, every effort, every contribution . . . goes into transfiguring the manner of execution, changing the language, and helping the spirit take a new step."

With Cézanne, the contemporary aspect of what de Kooning calls "trembling but very precisely" might make his credentials in the Empyrean of Piero and Vermeer seem questionable. But even the word "sensation" in this context comes from Cézanne as something realized in both his motif and the solidity of whatever examples he admired in the art of museums. (The fact that he admired the programmed classicism of Poussin is nearly beside the point.) To advance a naïve perfectionism as the issue in Cézanne, much less in Piero or Vermeer, is to sidestep the relevance of artistic truth. The aesthetic of still life is better translated as silence; *la vie silencieuse* was the indigenous French term. (*Nature morte* skulking in comes from Latin.) This stillness or silence is provisional, like the conception of a sentence as a complete thought. "Declarative" is one component of the surface; others are a silence as full as light, and a countenance that functions as a forward edge. The negative aspect would be "no frills" and nothing you could call purity, either. In his essay of Piero, Guston refers to a "a necessary and generous law." In so far as it's a state, it's discussible in the neighborhood of the word "sublime."

Sublime has a funny history. Without using it, but maybe gainsaying the local usage, Whitman mentioned his own "state of high exalted musing

. . . yet the senses not lost or counteracted." That's not the usual story of sublime. From Edmund Burke we are given to understand "If the object is both simple and vast, the eye (and therefore the mind) does not arrive readily at its bounds, and has no rest, since the image is everywhere the same. Hence the impression of an artificial infinite is created by a large and unified object which throws the retina into tension and impresses itself so vividly on the mind that an idea of the sublime is suggested." This sublime seems destined, in effect, to devastate your concentration. But there's no such scatter in the actual word. From Greek through Latin origins carrying the prefix *sub* (under) along with *limen* (threshold or lintel) or *limne* (coastal edge, bay or harbor), it's not readily seen how sublime got to mean generally "high" or "lofty," or otherwise not containable, contained. Strangely, it seems the earliest recorded usage took it as "lofty," and only later did the word get returned to a literal physical base. Well, "lofty" under the lintel of sky: the Egyptian hieroglyph for sky resembles "a horizontal architectural member supporting the weight above an opening." *Sublimated* as a gas raised to produce a refined product: but *subliminal* "applied to states supposed to exist but not strong enough to be recognized." In psychology, *limen* now means "the limit below which a stimulus ceases to be visible" and refers also to the Greek *leimon* (meadow). "Liminality" is "the threshold or initial stage of a process," the *limen* past indifference, or "liminal intensity of sensation." Hold it right there. In Latin, hem, fringe, *limbus*, e.g. Limbo (fringe, meadow) of Hell, "a border distinguished by color or structure or both." The limbic system of the brain is a group of subcortical structures supposedly concerned with emotion and motivation.

Chaucer used "sublime" in the sense of vapors. Edmund Spenser took it to mean "proud." Longinus called his book on oratory *Peri Hupsous,* a fair translation of which would be *On High Style or Literary Excellence.* In 1674, the French academic poet Boileau, who combed his sources for literary statutes, circulated his *Traité du Sublime ou du Merveilleux dans le Discours Traduit du Grec de Longin,* and where he got *sublime* or how it developed more international currency than *le merveilleux,* who knows? Boileu and his sublime were immediately popular in England: so fashionable that, by 1728, Pope wrote a parody called *Peri Bathous, or the Art of Sinking in Poetry.* But Burke's usage, and the later English conception of the sublime in view of landscape, was different. Burke expounded terror, revulsion, a vertigo or point of no return, when faced with nature's marvels—but allowing (in fact, guaranteeing) complete aesthetic satisfaction if taken at a convenient distance, from behind say, the guard rail of Niagara Falls. The rest of the story you probably know: Immanuel Kant's versions ("mathematical" and "dynamic"), "when we seek in a single intuition to gather up the aggregates into one; when, in a word, we seek to realize by reason this magnitude, we transcend every standard of sense and the feeling of the sublime is evoked." The ideas of magnitude entertained by Burke and Kant were strangely limited given the close-observation sciences of their time that showed any-sized entities to be epideictic. Incidentally, it was Napoleon the First who said, "From the sublime to the ridiculous is but a single step"—on the occasion of his retreat through devastating ice and snow and mud from Moscow.

So etymology is a kind of crystal text, a transit system you can travel and get almost anywhere. Sublime may be an all-purpose, "everything" word; or if it does mean "lofty" that's fine too. It can modify an Alp, a poem, or the strange smile of a goof. But I listen harder when it's connected to those other sounds that keep rooting it back to physics—like "point," "threshold," "verge," "brink," "the brink of chaos," "ledge," "sill," et cetera. I hate to think we'd be left with "liminality" after all this.

Generally I find art lessons infused with scientism distasteful, unless the unison is confirmed. Light in painting might be equal to resonance in poems or the character of a tone, which aren't phonemes any more than light is iron oxide and titanium. Light and space are vector fields, and with gravity thrown in, the balance of matter, if you see balance, is a continual demarcation: let it go at that and call it a door. Most everyday observations are contributions in one way or another to physics. How you and the work look inside each other in aerial perspective from 30,000 feet should be dignified by your awareness too. Albert Einstein slipped into various theories discomforting to himself from "simply" wanting to know what light is, and gravity. The process of definition, finally, like with Freud, became an infinite dark one of going deep inside, like digging to China. The central impulse might reassert itself yet. This isn't specifically modern. Like seventeenth-century gentlemen scholars, Einstein or Freud could have sat up nights writing detailed verses descriptive of every invertebrate currently residing in the home, and giving each of them a fancy name: *Solly Hemus, Oniscus Sublimus, Norman Frame.*

If I have come close to identifying an ideal, I hope to have avoided conceit in telling of it. Actually, how anyone can stay true to anything, even remembering the dreams of youth, is beyond this guy's comprehension. I don't want to expend so many sentences on conceit, partly because it's all too generally recognizable and exploitive, and unless generously composted, desolate. It's conceit, rather than idealism, that registers as impossibly austere. It's the flip side too, where idealism rolls over and bares its throat to unwholesome self-reflection. The antisocial aspects are indicated by a letter from J. Robert Oppenheimer, thus:

> Up to now, and even more in the days of my almost infinitely prolonged adolescence, I hardly took any action, hardly did anything, or failed to do anything, whether it was a paper on physics, or a lecture, or how I read a book, how I talked to a friend, how I loved, that did not arouse in me a very great sense of revulsion and of wrong.
>
> It turned out to be impossible for me to live with anybody else, without understanding that what I saw was only one part of the truth, and in an attempt to break out and be a reasonable man. I had to realize that my own worries about what I did were valid and were important, but that they were not the whole story, that there must be a complimentary way of looking at them, because other people did not see them as I did. And I needed what they saw, needed them.

The same sense of wrong may keep a poet from his work, making himself self-reflexive/critical rather than the work. *Sic transit* the role conceit plays in forgetting to show for induction. Elsewise, "sit down solitary and scary and work the words out"? In his three-by-five pocket notebook, Whitman copied out his own certified mail, and presuming an apodictic snarl, "It says, sarcastically, Walt you understand enough . . . Why don't you let it out them?" What did Walt write down next? "Seas of bright juice suffuse heaven." Whitman and Dante let you know to what degree they participate in the work without necessarily assuming the role of prime mover.

Conceit is a corruption of the original flash that actuality has substance rather than being "the void between events." What he saw in the moment he did in a flash, or: "There is probably more than one way of proceeding but of course you want only the one way that is denied you." The wholeness I see in painting and poetry is often inaccessible to me in music because my ears aren't fast enough to take the whole score as structure. I hear notes, and can realize the wholeness of each note as in, say Mozart or Thelonious Monk. But any structure larger than thirty-two bars is likely to go by as only a parade of details. I want something to steady the score. Relief comes, however, in the notion that in some music (maybe Mozart, but I've been told this about Schoenberg and Bach) the details do contain the whole—as if shattered into a million bits, will still produce the entire image out of any single piece. Dante said the canzone worked on the same principle, containing the whole art, like the Empyrean that "has in itself, in every part that which its matter desires."

Melancholy conceit: "Those lowly creatures that have gone to sleep out of sheer laziness. The melancholia (in fact, an angel artist), on the contrary, is . . . super-awake; her fixed stare is one of intent though fruitless searching. She is inactive not because she is too lazy to work but because work has become meaningless to her; her energy is paralyzed not by sleep but by thought." *Geo ponderat*—the weight of the world? "Former melancholics had been unfortunate misers and sluggards, despised for their unsociability and general incompetence." Temporary relief may be obtained from tai chi, regular hours, Adele Davis, concert going, and plans to save the world; semiotics, a last resort. Panofsky writes of the artistic melancholia of past times as "surrounded by the halo of the sublime."

Any carpenter knows the tedium of remodeling a structure that by rights ought to be hauled away. There's the work and there are odd jobs.

Maintenance as it happens in a poetic community often takes a form of clever conceit, but it can also posit sincerity against the brassbound logics that spit historical imperatives like nails. The trouble with a lot of exclusively novelty-minded writing is that it leans on its defenses, and its defenses are made of the kind of debased figures of speech that the poems at best would refuse. Maintenance threatens to congeal into satire (sly rap), fixed character and disappointed or gnarled ideals. When the disappointed idealist thinks of civilization, "I see 'no-no's," he says.

When George Balanchine died, one close friend, a filmmaker, saw it as the end of civilization; another narrowed the premise saying the nineteenth century had definitively drawn to a close. One eulogist said rightly that Balanchine had led "a completely manifest life." That perennial question of moment: Can we have it all? "On the death of some men the world reverts to ignorance" (Wallace Stevens). Edwin Denby's amused and passionate assertions about art as a civilized activity as well as a natural (and maddening) one were anomalous. But he was really amazingly firm and light-handed about them. Imagine an erudite contemporary in this world taking the stance that particular genius is general (standard operational, as it were) and that shit is simply off the beam. Such an attitude helps push away scads of nonsense. Ordinarily, any positive avowal of "civilization" is bound to be aggressive. There are no unguarded assertions on that score. I like to think of "civilized" as a term of endearment that's approximately functional, shaped between one and one or not at all. *Civility* anyhow, where you talk like somebody with an energetic world view, and not some monkey on the moon, or a tired killer. Trying to say "civilized" to an audience of unknown quantities—I mean, try it with a roomful of sixth graders: if you're nervous about it, the tone will bear no relation and you'll get laughed off the boards. I read Denby's lines on flying over the historical Mediterranean in conjunction with a regulatory thought from Whitehead:

And fifty years hence will he love Rome in place of me?
For it is with regret I leave the lovely world men made
Despite their bad character, their art is mild.

And Whitehead's thought:

> Consciousness itself is the product of art in its lowliest form . . . In
> a sense art is a morbid overgrowth of functions which lie deep in
> nature. It is the essence of art to be artificial. But it is its perfection
> to return to nature, remaining art. In short art is the education of
> nature. Thus, in its broadest sense, art is civilization.

When Edwin spoke to ballet students about the audience end of performance, he discussed the sort of seeing "that leads to recognizing on
stage and inside yourself an echo of some personal, original excitement
you already know . . . the event which originally caused the excitement
is not literally the same as the events you see happen on stage." I'd like
to suggest that the distinction between an artist's "prime style" and his
"mediating style," which Carter Ratcliff made recently in reference to
Cézanne, can be augmented by overlaying parallels of that "original
excitement" echo and the idealism I've tried to signify. Carter sometimes
uses "pure" in place of "prime" but I'm going to stick with prime:

> The first—the prime style, the vehicle of the artist's meaning for
> him- or herself—is generated from the most inward aspects of
> the artist's own experience. The second—which could be called a
> mediating style—does what can be done to make the necessarily
> elusive meanings of the prime style available to an audience. Most
> artworks blend prime and mediating styles. The maturity of a great
> artist renders the blending seamless . . . The artist whose mediat-
> ing style dominates—or crushes—the inward aspects of his art is
> of course much more familiar these days than the artist who—like
> Cézanne—seems not to care much if his art is understood and, not
> caring, puts little effort into the improvement of his mediating style.
> Nonetheless, Cézanne's images are filled with devices intended to
> mediate between his most elusive meanings and his audience's
> habits of vision. It's just that his elusiveness . . . dominates. For that
> reason—because, in other words, Cézanne was so little concerned
> to ingratiate himself—many of the New York audience of the late
> '70s were exasperated.

Well, Carter's and my estimations of Cézanne's elusiveness differ. But the point is that the prime/pure style could just as well represent the artist's idealism antecedent to, or in, process, and that the blend of prime and mediating style is the vehicle by which, "seamless," the artist both passes on his ideal and extends, or ostends, it in some unique way. This is what, in practice, "tradition" is—a continual chain of links going in-out-in-out-in—though maybe the Buddhist term "transmitting" is more exact. This passing on is an event something like waves or rays. The audience I imagine here, though certainly not always, would be different from the art-world one Carter is so right about. I'm back with that kid of John Thorpe's and his original encounter of a kind that patently didn't come from nowhere. The correlative is found in Edwin Denby's sonnet:

> At fifteen maybe believed the world
> Would turn out so honorable
> So much like what poetry told
> Heartbreak and heroes of fable
> And so it did; close enough; the
> Djin gave it, disappeared laughing.

The Poetry Project, St. Marks in the Bowery Church, 1984

Sources of quotation and/or allusion: Osip Mandelstam, Joseph Anthony Masseo, Ted Berrigan, Clark Coolidge, William Carlos Williams, Dante Alighieri, John Thorpe, Jack Spicer, Erwin Panofsky, Wallace Stevens, Adrian Stokes, Samuel Edgerton, Francis Ponge, Philip Hendy, Philip Guston, Juan Gris, Henri Focillon, Alex Katz, Willem de Kooning, Morton Feldman, Albert Blankert, John Montias, Roberto Longhi, Paul Cézanne, Samuel H. Monk, *Oxford Dictionary of the English Language*, J. Robert Oppenheimer, Alfred North Whitehead, Justin Kaplan, Walt Whitman, John Ashbery, Tom Clark, Edwin Denby, Carter Ratcliff.

4

The title of this talk is "History and Truth," which may sound beyond preposterous for a brief commencement chat, but what I mean to do is lay out somewhat breezily some of my own diversity of purpose in the face of such enormous abstractions—and hopefully those will seem less daunting, more congenial by the time I've finished.

"Diversity"—because it can only be an allowance of diversity that got me here to address you today. I failed to ask Anne Wagner, when she called, if I was being invited to talk as a poet, a critic or an art-historian-without-portfolio (which is what I am, at best and gladly, in that department). So I don't know what she or Tim Clark or anyone may have had in mind by asking me. It can't be that I am standing here as just, so to speak, my bare self, flagrantly denuded of any degree of official representation. In truth, I know myself to be representative of no official order. I also know I agreed to do this because when Anne said the date "May 24th" I immediately thought of the first book of poems by a favorite poet, James Schuyler's *May 24th or So*, and a line in that book that goes:

You can't get at a sunset naming colors.

So, a pause here for naming oneself, for convenient identity control— just to get *me* out of the way: Primarily, I am a writer—a poet who, as the art magazines say in their notes on contributors, "also writes about art." Early in my poet's life, 1960 or so, I slipped on a banana peel and began writing art criticism. The impetus was roughly that I wanted to avoid the fate then typical for American poets, which was to teach literature and/or creative writing in some small college far from where one wanted to be, which in my case was my hometown of New York. The working model for poets writing about contemporary art was conspicuous among New York poets like John Ashbery, Frank O'Hara, Barbara Guest and Jimmy Schuyler. (Could you tell that Schuyler was an art critic from his line about a sunset?) There was an honorable local tradition, and it seemed to fit; so, like several of my peers in the second-generation New York School, I followed suit—until almost ten years later, with big changes in the art world (and particularly in the practice of criticism), the impetus wore thin. Moving to California in 1970, I abruptly left off, an art-world dropout. Then again, another fifteen years down the line, primarily on the strength of my New York background, I found myself hired to teach art history at the San Francisco Art Institute. As bananas go, this was stray peel number two—and as I was in dire need of steady employment at the time, I appreciated the chance to slip on it.

That takes care of my history to the extent that most of what I just told you is true. Is history an account of verifiable fact? The rest of this talk—in the form of ruminations (literally, grazing the topic)—follows from a set of epigraphs, two from Gertrude Stein, one from Robert Smithson:

The last line of Stein's "If I Told Him: A Completed Portrait of Picasso," completed in 1923, reads:

Let me recite what history teaches. History teaches.

Joining this in my mind is the last line of Stein's 1929 opera libretto *Four Saints in Three Acts*, chanted emphatically by the full chorus in Virgil Thomson's setting. That line goes:

Which is a fact.

(Which I've always felt to be the great, perfect exit line for just about *anything*.)

Lastly, Robert Smithson's admonition, written many years later, in the late 1960s:

All clear ideas tend to be wrong.

As a poet, as an art writer and in my dippings into art history—in those activities altogether—I find I am nearly crazy about facts. A slide of a painting is a clear idea, photographically conveyed, and a poor—though teachable—representation of observable fact. As Alex Katz likes to say, a slide of a painting gives you no scale, no surface, no light and the color's all wrong—so what you get is a graphic anomaly. No slides today. Instead, I'll drop a poem or two in the slot. My poems are often the result of searching out facts regarding this or that name or word or thing—but I will also be the first to admit that I have an uncertain idea about what constitutes a fact beyond a fair notion of the possibility that something is, or has been, the case. An image of the case. A piece of Robert Creeley's goes: "You want / the fact / of things / in words / of words."

What is so appealing about a fact is often its inconsequentiality. Beyond the relief that somehow astonishingly there are words for what it tells you, there is the temptation to leave a fact at its own face value. Let the statement, observation or description, as the case may be, hang in the air as-is. Art historians know only too well how, and with what regularity, their eager colleagues' shrewd interpretations bring about sets of corrupted fact. Some facts, I believe, exhibit their true colors best by remaining beautifully, resolutely pointless. Authoritative history, however, has no appetite for pointless stories; thus, each fact is liable to be confronted with a preemptive glare or squint, the Muse of History's vast, groaning, imperious "So What?" Without that "what" there's nothing teachable.

Here is a poem that resulted from discovering in an otherwise dull book two or three things about the philosopher Denis Diderot and his family—facts rubbed together in a way that I think of as igniting a small, sly fire in the language. It's called "The Recital":

THE RECITAL

It is said that, late in life, Denis Diderot force-fed his wife Nanette a diet of R-rated poetry and fiction, including his own *Jacques the Fatalist*, as a cure for her feelings of moral superiority. Diderot read to Nanette morning, noon and night, and whenever the Diderots had company, Mrs. D. would recite to her visitors whatever she had just absorbed. Slowly but surely, the cure took. "Conversation doubles the effect of the dosage," in a letter to their daughter wrote Diderot.

W.H. Auden wrote, "Culture is history which has become dormant or extinct, a second nature." Generally, the modern idea of history is a way of coping with, by accounting for, our tantalizingly unstable culture—to give events leading up to the present a look of logical development, where really there is none. Turnover, shock—or its corollary, resentment—is neither development nor revolt; it's our vernacular status quo. Logic masks a chaos which may be friendlier than the logic espoused to shield us from it. During his October 1986 talk on Hans Hofmann across this campus at the Berkeley Art Museum, Clement Greenberg spoke of how "Hofmann's paintings . . . had the habit of faring better with time. His works never looked as bad, if they did look bad, as they did the first time you saw them. Ever after they got better."

This remark, a variety of dialectical upside-down cake, is in fact an accurate account of the average viewer's experience with Hofmann's work—and not so incidentally states a view of history as perfectly, sensibly unstable and illogical. Even better is the artist Joe Brainard's way of dispensing with Greenberg's hothouse problem over badness and getting straight to the point. In a letter to an older artist friend, Joe wrote, "What I like about Hans Hofmann is that he is hard to like." Such a remark appeals to the more open-air vicissitudes of art as a variety of social behavior, from which aesthetic experience should never be thought to be exempt.

Art historical logic, museological practice or the arguments of art critics are good as long they direct us back to the works under discussion with their facts illuminated, and they are bad when they direct us away from the work in favor of an overarching—and sense-stultifying—idea. In 1966 the critic Gene Swenson remarked: "The theory of Cubism is more visible than the paintings themselves." My daughter Siobhan, who never studied art history but who likes to look at pictures, visited the Museum of Modern Art in New York for the first time in her mid-twenties. There, standing flatfooted before a 1911 Picasso, she was non-plussed. Rushing to her aid, an older friend offered the conventional excuse that Picasso's Analytical Cubism was a way of painting objects as if seen from all sides at once, whereupon Siobhan shrugged, said "Bad idea!" and moved on.

"Bad idea!" covers a lot of territory. I love museums for what they permit me to see that otherwise I couldn't. But there is that type of museological thinking where art functions to flesh out only our "museum" idea of things—down the enfilades, as it were, phase by phase. Museums generally, for better or worse, are organized to help us see that way, to leave out what doesn't help maintain the perspective. (Presumably we would get lost without the logic.) Bad ideas enable you to move along. Good ones light up the occasion of seeing, often by contrast, but watch out, they might stop you in your tracks. Rudy Burckhardt's son Jacob is now himself a filmmaker like his late father. In Florence, at the age of two, he followed the prescribed route with his parents through the Uffizi. Seeing Botticelli's tall, blond Venus after nine galleries packed with Madonnas of various stripes, Jacob cried out in a fit of primal iconological ardor: "Nice clean lady—no baby!"

History is funny. Lately is it is full of what some recall as dearly departed afterlives. One day in the late 1980s David Antin said, "Depending on what you believe Modernism was, you get the Postmodernism you deserve." More recently, Hal Foster, one of the definers of Post-, wrote an essay called "Whatever Happened to Postmodernism?" Depending on what you believe Post- was, what now is our deservable present—or more to the point, our *desirable* one? I was fascinated, gladdened to hear that Tim Clark was giving two seminars this year—one in the work of Paul Cézanne, and another in Nicolas Poussin, who exemplified for Cézanne what he called "the art of the museums." As it happened, just as Tim's classes were steaming along, the contemporary painter Vija Celmins was quoted as saying: "What we need now is less Duchamp and more Cézanne." As if a Cézanne-esque art of tirelessly plunging perceptual sincerity—earthiness mixed with rag-tag spiritual gropings—had a prayer amid today's otherwise laudable (and entirely

Duchampian) skepticism and blitheness. If so, maybe we can now get back to our delicious chaos—our grand inconsequentiality.

The ardent lover of history proceeds toward knowing everything about a work of art even if all of the big original ideas about it get shredded in the process. One enjoys an art historian's tough—truly critical—love, wherein the work stays central and the historian's performance is a threading of her attentiveness—cultural, perceptual, lingual—around and through, making an orbit in kind. Frank O'Hara's most cogent political statement, "The only truth is face to face" serves by extension for the truth of art and poetry. Truth is face to face with every facet—or nuance—of fact. By nuance, every word of a poem gathers the poem's surface energy. By the nuance of its surface a painting we might call "great" actualizes its place in the culture that bred it.

My last fact for today follows on the sad, unsociable events of last September. A very short prose poem, it proposes to be not much more than an accurate account of its moment, but it seemed to me after having written it that whatever urgency or pertinence it holds is all in the nuance, including the slip of mistaken identity that got me going. Bare ideology, needy and resentful, has little patience with nuance. But it is exactly the subtler aspects of this historical reality that must be faced, and deeply felt, or else we continue to suffer the extremities. I hope that, at one reading, this poem's anti- or *meta*-ideological stance is plain:

GLORIA

A large U.S. flag flaps loudly outside our dining room, suspended on a pole from the topmost balcony across the way. I keep taking it for some poor thug running through the late September night, sneakers smacking.

Commencement Address, History of Art Department,
University of California, Berkeley, 2002

5

When Eric Athenot kindly invited me to be part of this conference, his invitation included the proposal that I "give a paper," which I instantly said I could not possibly do. "But," I wrote him, "I will happily read some Whitman and make remarks," and he replied that that would be OK. But here I have surprised myself—and hopefully not disappointed Eric or any of you—by concocting not exactly a "paper" but the connecting of some dots appropriate to this occasion—a celebration of Whitman's *Leaves of Grass* in Paris (where in fact at age 18 I bought my first little paperback Whitman, at George Whitman's bookshop on the Quai St. Michel)—some notions, followed by a few poems by others and a part of one by Whitman himself.

There are a couple of epigraphs, both from *An American Primer* or *The Primer of Words*, which Whitman wrote in 1850-56, but which was published only posthumously, in 1904:

> What do you think words are? Do you think words are positive and original things in themselves—No; words are not original and arbitrary in themselves—Words are a result—they are the progeny of what has been or is in vogue.

And:

> I like limber, lasting, fierce words—I like them applied to myself—I like them in newspapers, courts, debates, congress . . .

One way to read Whitman is as a Realist. When the poet John Thorpe says that Whitman in his poems speaks "real American ceremonial," I take most of the "ceremonial" there, and a large part of the "real," to be the newspaper rhetoric and political and religious oratory of the

United States in the mid-1800s. Such sources would of course include Whitman's direct engagement as a printer, an editor and frontline journalist, and his attentive, closely discriminate hearing of such public speakers as Abraham Lincoln, the preacher/reformer Henry Ward Beecher, the radical Republican Robert Ingersoll, and the Quaker Elias Hicks. Justin Kaplan tells us that to write *Leaves of Grass* Whitman "undid his bundle of manuscripts and clippings and drew out materials." Whitman himself tells of the voice that goaded him, saying "sarcastically: Walt, you understand enough . . . Why don't you let it out then?"

In its materials, Realism's perennial radicality always seems to involve perception of more than people and things in their contemporary everyday look; just as daringly, it takes on the concomitant facts of representation—replaying common language and imagery to get at what's happening in the world in a recognizable manner. Realism has to account for what is real. Words and usage are real. In painting, paint is real. "The flash associated with advertising" became the light in a 1960s New Realist painting. "Commercial art is not our art," said Roy Lichtenstein, speaking for the new-realist Pop artists of the time. "It is our subject matter and in that sense it is nature."

> The greatest poet hardly knows pettiness or triviality. If he breathes into anything that was before thought small it dilates with the grandeur and life of the universe. (*Preface* to the 1855 edition)

Modern Realism begins in painting with Courbet, who painted his *Stonebreakers* the same year Whitman began his *Primer* and whose show "Le Réalisme" opened in the Paris Exposition of (guess when) 1855, an event that Whitman may well have heard about. Whitman's favorite painting was *The Sower* by Millet, inspirer of Vincent Van Gogh who later wrote his brother Theo praising the spirituality of *Leaves of Grass*. Courbet never painted Whitman who never left America—it fell to the Paris-trained American realist Thomas Eakins to accomplish that—but Courbet and the other great French realist Edouard Manet painted Whitman's great contemporary (two years his junior, born 1821) Charles Baudelaire. (Courbet's studio allegory with Baudelaire's portrait on the far right side was the newly completed centerpiece of the 1855 exhibition.)

Seas of bright juice suffuse heaven. Not an Alexandrine, not mellifluous, not a classical line at all. *Leaves of Grass, Fleurs du Mal*—what a euphonious odd couple they make. Whitman embodies Baudelaire's injunction to plunge "au fond du gouffre pour trouver le nouveau." But does any green grass grow in Baudelaire's "forests of symbols"? *Les Fleurs* followed *Leaves* into print in 1857, as did *Madame Bovary* by the self-proclaimed Realist, Gustave Flaubert. All three ran afoul of the censors and became much-maligned authors of "dirty" books. Like Whitman, before his poetry appeared, Baudelaire was known primarily as a journalist—in his case, an art critic. Whitman and Baudelaire were the two most photographed nineteenth-century writers. Nadar made his first portrait photograph of Baudelaire in 1855, at which point Baudelaire was engrossed in translating Edgar Allan Poe, about whom Walt had mixed feelings, as he probably had apropos Baudelaire, if indeed he knew anything of Baudelaire's work.

Baudelaire and Whitman shared an uncanny alertness to, if wildly divergent attitudes toward, "the heroism of modern life." Walt's pragmatism was at one with his "high, exalted musing"; he and Baudelaire were extraordinarily quick to recognize that modernity presented an irrevocably altered situation, and were insistent about envisioning it (for better and worse) in the grandest possible, apodictic terms. They were the first true modern city poets. As much as Baudelaire, Whitman in his twenties assumed the stance of metropolitan dandy, observing "million-footed Manhattan," loving (more than Baudelaire ever would) "the blab of the pave," the "superb music" of street talk. Whitman's eagerness is apposite, not contradictory, to Baudelaire's exquisite disgust, but intoxication by shocks of sheer mass (mainly people in crowds) is common to both Whitman's rowdy democratic vision and Baudelaire's aristocracy *d'esprit*. Both are, as Walter Benjamin would say, *clochards*, tireless, solitary collectors of worlds; the difference is in Baudelaire's embrace of alienation ("anywhere but here, anytime but now") and Whitman's circumvention of it. Whitman contradicted himself and contained "multitudes"; Baudelaire was known as a ham actor socially who changed personas at will.

"What have I for my poems? I have all to make." Whitman was an avant-garde interloper; like Rimbaud, coming from the wrong circumstances, self-invented, he had no business writing verse. Yet, by the 1850s when *Leaves* came out, it had fallen to Whitman to enhance the vigor and scale of poetry in English, which had been languishing since the deaths of Shelley and Keats some thirty years previous. Indeed, Whitman acted like a steroid in this respect. After the 1880s—when English poetry had been reduced to varieties of slur and sputtering (think Swinburne for the first, Tennyson for the second)—the only other reinvigoration came from the French: from Corbiére, Nerval, Rimbaud, Laforgue (Laforgue was the first to translate Whitman into French), and eventually the likes of Apollinaire, Reverdy, Breton and Char.

Courbet used newspaper etchings for the basic design of *Bonjour, Monsieur Courbet*—casting himself in the popular image of the Wandering Jew. In the 1960s, New Realists looked hard at and absorbed into their art comics, billboards, movie posters and other types of commercial graphic design, mostly centered on photographic imagery. The point for them (as for Whitman, I believe) was a fast and effective meaning-delivery system based on collective recognitions. The admonition in Whitman's *Primer* "Be simple and clear—be not occult" might be found just as well in Andy Warhol's *ABCs*. And counter-clockwise, we can hear Walt saying, alongside Andy, "If you want to know all about [me] just look at the surface of my [poems], and there I am. There's nothing behind it."

In 1962 the Sidney Janis Gallery in New York mounted a wonderful, and then somewhat scandalous, show called The New Realism—it was the first, and perhaps only, show of the time to combine work by European and American artists working in modes related to what soon after would be known as Pop. (The name, of course, came from Pierre Restany's typification of Yves Klein, Arman, Martial Raysse, Tinguely, Mimmi Rotella etc. as *Nouveaux Réalistes*.) In the handout text for the show, John Ashbery wrote of the objects dealt with by the international New Realist artists as "a common ground, a neutral language understood by everybody and therefore the ideal material with which to create experiences which transcend."

Now I'll get to the point, and on to some poems:

For the type of heightened Realism Whitman practiced, diction is the key. As light is the voice of painting, diction is the light of poetry. It is also the means of Whitman's forced entry into great poetry and his staying power. "Pronunciation is the stamina of language," he writes (again in the *Primer*). In his biography of Whitman, Kaplan makes just enough, I think, of how much of Whitman's bright, if sometimes blaring, diction derived from the smart talk of journalese, but of course there is the vastness of his reference field—literary, idiomatic, technical—as unrestricted as one could wish.

It is the sense of an endlessly inventive, existentially appropriate diction that Whitman bequeaths. Or maybe that is just what great poetry does, and why on opening the works of certain poets we instantly feel the presence of that possibility surging from the page. Whitman certainly is an instance of that. Confronting him, I feel I can say, as Bernadette Mayer says of her own poetry, "It's as if the language wants to say this"—and so it does.

For the time remaining, I'm going to read, with barely any commentary, a sequence of poems by American poets that exemplify a particularity and expansiveness of diction identifiable in very different ways as "Whitmanesque"—maybe especially because the inflections in American language have changed so immensely, by phases, in the past 150 years.

Here, for openers, is William Carlos Williams in an idiom largely unheard anymore, from 1917:

DANSE RUSSE

If when my wife is sleeping
and the baby and Kathleen
are sleeping
and the sun is a flame-white disc
in silken mists

above shining trees,—
if I in my north room
dance naked, grotesquely
before my mirror
waving my shirt round my head
and singing softly to myself:
"I am lonely, lonely,
I was born to be lonely,
I am best so!"
If I admire my arms, my face,
my shoulders, flanks, buttocks
against the yellow drawn shades, —

Who shall say I am not
the happy genius of my household?

Next: a poem from Charles Reznikoff's *Testimony: The United States 1885-1900*—written in the years 1941-59 but taken from court records of at least sixty years previous:

from TESTIMONY: THE UNITED STATES 1885-1900

Ten or twelve colored men
were gambling in the basement of a saloon on State Street—
rolling dice,
sitting or standing on opposite sides of a table.
Scott was playing
and Luther keeping track of the bets.

Calhoun shoved a dime over to pay a man called "Kentuck";
it got mixed in with Scott's money,
and Calhoun reached forward to grab it.
Scott said: "Do you want to rob me?"
At that Luther spoke up,
lifting the little stick he held in his hand,
"Let me explain it to you, Scott."

"I don't want you to explain it to me."
"But I will explain it to you."
"I don't care for you to explain anything to me."
"I want to tell you . . ."
"I don't want you to tell me."
"Let me show you how it is."
"I don't want you to show me."
"You need not talk that way, Scott.
I have always been a friend to you."
"And I don't give a damn for you."

Luther leaned back in his chair
and put his hands on the railing of the table.
"There's more people in this town cares for me
than I do for them.
I will show you what I care for you,"
and he got up
and threw the little stick down.

Scott had been picking up his money with his right hand.
He put the money in his pocket
and when his hand came out
it held a pistol.
"And I'll show you how much I care for you," he said
and shot Luther.

Frank O'Hara, as Olivier Brossard demonstrated just an hour ago, is a
poet after Whitman's heart:

RHAPSODY

515 Madison Avenue
door to heaven? portal
stopped realities and eternal licentiousness
or at least the jungle of impossible eagerness
your marble is bronze and your lianas elevator cables
swinging from the myth of ascending

I would join
or declining the challenges of racial attractions
they zing on (into the lynch, dear friends)
while everywhere love is breathing draftily
like a doorway linking 53rd with 54th
the east-bound with the west-bound traffic by 8,000,000s
o midtown tunnels and the tunnels, too, of Holland

where is the summit where all aims are clear
the pin-point light upon a fear of lust
as agony's needlework grows up around the unicorn
and fences him for milk—and yoghurt-work
when I see Gianni I know he's thinking of John Ericson
playing the Rachmaninoff 2nd or Elizabeth Taylor
taking sleeping-pills and Jane thinks of Manderley
and Irkutsk while I cough lightly in the smog of desire
and my eyes water achingly imitating the true blue

a sight of Manahatta in the towering needle
multi-faceted insight of the fly in the stringless labyrinth
Canada plans a higher place than the Empire State Building
I am getting into a cab at 9th Street and 1st Avenue
And the Negro driver tells me about a $120 apartment
"where you can't walk across the floor after 10 at night
not even to pee, cause it keeps them awake downstairs"
no, I don't like that "well I didn't take it"
perfect in the hot humid morning on my way to work
a little supper-club conversation for the mill of the gods

you were there always and you know all about these things
as indifferent as an encyclopedia with your calm brown eyes
it isn't enough to smile when you run the gauntlet
you've got to spit like Niagara Falls on everybody or
Victoria Falls or at least the beautiful urban fountains of Madrid
as the Niger joins the Gulf of Guinea near the Menemsha Bar
that is what you learn in the early morning passing Madison Avenue
where you've never spent any time and stores eat up light

I have always wanted to be near it
though the day is long (and I don't mean Madison Avenue)
lying in the hammock on St. Mark's Place sorting my poems
in the rancid nourishment of this mountainous island
they are coming and we holy ones must go
is Tibet historically a part of China? as I historically
belong to the enormous bliss of American death

And, complimentary to O'Hara, John Ashbery takes Whitman into the
domain of abstract emotion:

A BLESSING IN DISGUISE

Yes, they are alive and can have those colors,
But I, in my soul, am alive too.
I feel I must sing and dance, to tell
Of this in a way, that knowing you may be drawn to me.

And I sing amid despair and isolation
Of the chance to know you, to sing of me
Which are you. You see,
You hold me up to the light in a way

I should never have expected, or suspected, perhaps
Because you always tell me I am you,
And right. The great spruces loom.
I am yours to die with, to desire.

I cannot ever think of me, I desire you
For a room in which the chairs ever
Have their backs turned to the light
Inflicted on the stone and paths, the real trees

That seem to shine at me through a lattice toward you.
If the wild light of this January day is true
I pledge me to be truthful unto you
Whom I cannot ever stop remembering.

Remembering to forgive. Remember to pass beyond you into the day.
On the wings of the secret you will never know.
Taking me from myself, in the path
Which the pastel girth of the day has assigned to me.

I prefer "you" in the plural, I want "you,"
You must come to me, all golden and pale
Like the dew and the air.
And then I start getting this feeling of exaltation.

By now, hopefully, you get what I mean by diction and its distinctions. Here is Bernadette Mayer, in an erotic key, inside of which I can just about hear Whitman sighing and chortling. In fact, I'm going to let Walt join her without delay at the end, so that they can exit together waltzing:

FIRST TURN TO ME . . .

First turn to me after a shower,
you come inside me sideways as always

in the morning you ask me to be on top of you,
then we take a nap, we're late for school

you arrive at night inspired and drunk,
there is no reason for our clothes

we take a bath and lie down facing each other,
then later we turn over, finally you come

we face each other and talk about childhood
as soon as I touch your penis I wind up coming

you stop by in the morning to say hello
we sit on the bed indian fashion not touching

in the middle of the night you come home
from a nightclub, we don't get past the bureau

next day it's the table, and after that the chair
because I want so much to sit you down & suck your cock

you ask me to hold your wrists, but then when I
touch your neck with both my hands you come

it's early morning and you decide to very quietly
come on my knee because of the children

you've been away at school for centuries, your girlfriend
has left you, you come four times before morning

you tell me you masturbated in the hotel before you came by
I don't believe it, I serve the lentil soup naked

I massage your feet to seduce you, you are reluctant,
my feet wind up at your neck and ankles

you try not to come too quickly
also, you dont want to have a baby

I stand up from the bath, you say turn around
and kiss the backs of my legs and my ass

you suck my cunt for a thousand years, you are weary
at last I remember my father's anger and I come

you have no patience and come right away
I get revenge and won't let you sleep all night

we make out for so long we can't remember how
we wound up hitting our heads against the wall

I lie on my stomach, you put one hand under me
and one hand over me and that way can love me

you appear without notice and with flowers
I fall for it and we become missionaries

you say you can only fuck me up the ass when you are drunk
so we try it sober in a room at the farm

we lie together one night, exhausted couplets
and don't make love. does this mean we've had enough?

watching t.v. we wonder if each other wants to
interrupt the plot; later I beg you to read to me

like the Chinese we count 81 thrusts
then 9 more out loud till we both come

I come three times before you do
and then it seems you're mad and never will

it's only fair for a woman to come more
think of all the times they didn't care

• • •

from *The Sleepers*

8

The sleepers are very beautiful as they lie unclothed,
They flow hand in hand over the whole earth from east to west as
    they lie unclothed;

The Asiatic and African are hand in hand . . . the European and
    American are hand in hand,
Learned and unlearned are hand in hand . . . and male and female
    are hand in hand;
The bare arm of the girl crosses the bare breast of her lover . . .
    they press close without lust . . . his lips press her neck,
The father holds his grown or ungrown son in his arms with
    measureless love . . . and the son holds the father in his arms
    with measureless love,

The white hair of the mother shines on the white wrist of the
daughter,
The breath of the boy goes with the breath of the man . . . friend
is inarmed by friend,
The scholar kisses the teacher and the teacher kisses the scholar
. . . the wronged is made right,
The call of the slave is one with the master's call . . . and the
master salutes the slave,
The felon steps forth from the prison . . . the insane becomes sane
. . . the suffering of sick persons is relieved,
The sweatings and fevers stop . . . the throat that was unsound is
sound . . . the lungs of the consumptive are resumed . . . the
poor distressed head is free,
The joints of the rheumatic move as smoothly as ever, and
smoother than ever,
Stiflings and passages open . . . the paralysed become supple,
The swelled and convulsed and congested awake to themselves in
condition,
They pass the invigoration of the night and the chemistry of the
night and awake.

I too pass from the night;
I stay awhile away O night, but I return to you again and love you;
Why should I be afraid to trust myself to you?
I am not afraid . . . I have been well brought forward by you;
I love the rich running day, but I do not desert her in whom I
lay so long:
I know not how I came of you, and I know not where I go with you
. . . but I know I came well and shall go well.

I will stop only a time with the night . . . and rise betimes.
I will duly pass the day O my mother and duly return to you;
Not you will yield forth the dawn again more surely than you will
yield forth me again,
Not the womb yields the babe in its time more surely than I shall
be yielded from you in my time.

Université Paris 7eme, 2005

for Olivier Brossard

> There's no way of looking at a work of art by itself. It's not self-evident—it needs a history; it needs a lot of talking about. It's part of a man's whole life.
>
> —Willem de Kooning
> *Sketchbook No. 1*, 1960

> "The Elegies [Robert Motherwell's] mean something, and you can't beat that."
>
> —Frank O'Hara
> "Art Chronicle," *Kulchur*, Spring 1963

I hope this talk will provide something of a useful commentary on what seems to me to be an unusually fraught and concomitantly fruitful year in Frank O'Hara's history. I'm going to talk about just three poems and also read each aloud, the point being not to explicate so much as to place them, not to ferret out sources and meanings but to see to some extent what these poems do and in what circumstances they do it.

By way of preface, I want to address briefly the phenomenon of "Frank O'Hara at 80," which is being celebrated this year. Frank O'Hara was born in 1926, a good year for births, it turns out: Marilyn Monroe, Allen Ginsberg, Robert Creeley, Wallace Berman, Joan Mitchell, Fidel Castro, Tony Bennett, Chuck Berry, Miles Davis, John Coltrane, Michel Foucault, Morton Feldman . . . Pretty good for openers, no? Doubtless, there are more.

One of the three poems of O'Hara's I'm going to read is the one he began on his thirtieth birthday, June 27, 1956 and concluded four days later, on July 1st. The issue of June 27 being only a putative birth date—that, unbeknownst to Frank, his municipally recorded birth date was three months earlier—March 27 of that year, in Baltimore—is charming but literally, practically irrelevant: the June date was fixed in O'Hara's consciousness and appears as such, as actual in his poems, although he probably would been overjoyed to know the cause of that particular ruse, i.e., that his cautious Irish Catholic parents worked it to hide the fact that he was secretly illegitimate, a "love child."

I to you and you to me the endless oceans of

The notable years in a writer's life are sometimes singular, more often clustered. A few years ago in a lecture to art students Alex Katz suggested that any painter had three years to be on the cutting edge of style, "to be hip." This presupposes a kind of economic cycle, and poetry, being less economically determined, doesn't work that way. Poets can afford to be less style conscious than painters. By the time he turned 30, Frank had been writing poetry for at least ten years. The earliest surviving poem (first up in a sheaf entitled "Poems" from 1949) is dated October 13, 1946, early in his second year at Harvard. Thus, 1956, ten years before Frank died, was the exact midpoint of his literary life. It wasn't an especially prolific year—a fair number of poems (35), but most of them awfully slight or unusually tentative—but at least two of them ushered in what was incontestably the best and most extensive phase, lasting four or five years, of his work. 1956 wasn't 1959, the miracle year for Frank's poetry—42 poems, almost every one of which continues to be staggering in its beauty and invention.

The year in question is decisive, as any might be, but certain poems make it pointedly so. That framing things chronologically can be unwholesome is part of the message in these poems, so let's try to keep in mind the wider expanse. There's a lavish progression of what Ezra Pound would call "gists and piths," I think, in the poems of the mid-1950s—from "The Harbormaster" (1954) and "My Heart" (November, 1955) on to "Sleeping on the Wing," and further. In a note to Donald Allen, James Schuyler tells how Frank wrote "Sleeping on the Wing" just before New Year's, December 29, 1955: "The day this was written I was having breakfast (i.e. coffee) with Frank and Joe at 326 East 49th Street, and the talk turned to Frank's unquenchable inspiration, in a teasing way . . . The cigarette smoke began jetting from Frank's nostrils and he went in the next room and wrote 'Sleeping on the Wing' in a great clatter of keys."

SLEEPING ON THE WING

Perhaps it is to avoid some great sadness,
as in a Restoration tragedy the hero cries "Sleep!
O for a long sound sleep and so forget it!"
that one flies, soaring above the shoreless city,
veering upward from the pavement as a pigeon
does when a car honks or a door slams, the door
of dreams, life perpetuated in parti-colored loves
and beautiful lies all in different languages.

Fear drops away too, like the cement, and you
are over the Atlantic. Where is Spain? where is
who? The Civil War was fought to free the slaves,
was it? A sudden down-draught reminds you of gravity
and your position in respect to human love. But
here is where the gods are, speculating, bemused.
Once you are helpless, you are free, can you believe
that? Never to waken to the sad struggle of a face?
to travel always over some impersonal vastness,
to be out of, forever, neither in nor for!

The eyes roll asleep as if turned by the wind
and the lids flutter open slightly like a wing.
The world is an iceberg, so much is invisible!
and was and is, and yet the form, it may be sleeping
too. Those features etched in the ice of someone
loved who died, you are a sculptor dreaming of space
and speed, your hand alone could have done this.
Curiosity, the passionate hand of desire. Dead,
or sleeping? Is there speed enough? And, swooping,
you relinquish all that you have made your own,
the kingdom of your self sailing, for you must awake

and breathe your warmth in this beloved image
whether it's dead or merely disappearing,
as space is disappearing and your singularity.

The last stanza is a sonnet, fourteen lines, and the lines throughout lean toward rough Alexandrines but they're really just variables of anywhere from eleven to fourteen syllables. One could write a book on just that poem and how the terms of it—space, speed, "in," "for," sleeping and wakefulness, sculpture and personality, "and was and is"—carry into the textures of later work. I have a chart for just such a text, whereby some years ago I annotated every word—one page poem, nine pages of handwritten annotations, marvelously inconclusive. (You can't see them, at least not this evening.) But the poem is tremendously clear. The form—A/B/A—like a sonata. The mode is soliloquy, straight out of *Hamlet*. "I read Frank as a manual on how to live," Ted Berrigan once told me, and this is one of those telling instances, a poem to study for the thoughts it occasions about conditional life. At one point, I thought it must be about going crazy and then not going crazy. Kenneth Koch thought it was about dreaming. But really, though dreaming is part of it, it is about deciding, after some consultation with oneself, what one is to do, where and how: for the "I" and the ancillary, transformative "you" of this decision-making poem, one must live decisively "in" and "for," and not "out of," not in detached, impersonal space.

Frank's turning 30 begins in 1955. The change in his relations with Larry Rivers, already in the works in 1954, was crucial. Arguably, their love affair, on and off by then over five years, had stalled the development of their deeper mutual friendship, which pretty much stabilized around 1957, the time of their grandly affectionate hands-on collaboration, the lithographic portfolio *Stones*. Larry the "demented telephone" and Frank of the "gorgeous self pity," friends for life. In January, Frank was hired at the Museum of Modern Art as a special assistant in the International Program. In spring he submitted his manuscript—unlucky runner up, as it turned out—for the Yale Younger Poets award and soon after entered into the two-year process of working out with Grove Press what finally would be his first substantial book, *Meditations in an Emergency*. In June, Joe LeSueur moved in with him at East 49th

Street. At the end of September he was hit hard by the death of his screen love, James Dean, and over the next nine months wrote seven poems on the subject. In October he quit reviewing for *ArtNews* and in December learned that he had been awarded a Rockefeller grant to be poet-in-residence at the Poets Theater in Cambridge beginning in January of the coming year. In November he wrote the two major poems of 1955, "Sleeping on the Wing" and "To the Film Industry in Crisis" (the latter of which, oddly, does not mention James Dean at all). The six-month, winter-spring 1956 Cambridge stint proved depressing; a case of seemingly unremitting doldrums: few, mostly inconsequential poems, and nothing to show for the residency except for some brushing up on historical drama, reading at least three books by D.H. Lawrence and meeting the 22-year-old John Wieners and being introduced to Gregory Corso by Bunny Lang. O'Hara returned to New York by late June, having spent some interim weeks at George Montgomery's place in Sandwich, New Hampshire, reading *Remembrance of Things Past*.

> The objects of the Poet's thoughts are everywhere, though the eyes and sense of man are, it is true, his favorite guides, yet he will follow wheresoever he can find an atmosphere of sensation in which to move his wings . . .
> —William Wordsworth,
> Preface to *Lyrical Ballads* (1802)

"In Memory of My Feelings" runs about five pages in typescript and takes about twelve minutes to read. It has the feel of a long poem with both lyric and epic implications. The title suggests an elegy but, despite the high mortality rate, the many "kills" tallied or imminent within its scenic spread, the poem doesn't bear that out; it's best heard, I think, as an ode, as Whitman's "Song of Myself" is an ode, wild and oddly plotted. It's a real cliffhanger—a salvaging operation, it turns out—somewhat panicky, and some of the panic, I think, has to do with ambition in the face of mortality. At his birthday party the night of the same day the poem began—given by Grace Hartigan, to whom "In Memory of My Feelings" is dedicated—Frank wept wildly, considering the smallness of his achievement to date compared with those of Keats and Chatterton, both of whom had died well before reaching 30.

I believe that at least part of the impetus for "In Memory of My Feelings" was the sense of alarm occasioned by arriving at the age he was, along with a few contemporary reminders or goads—not least of which would have been the immediately discernible impact of Allen Ginsberg's "Howl," in circulation in New York by spring '56 by way of ditto copies typed in San Francisco by Robert Creeley. Not that Frank's work at the time was negligible, but he clearly felt it was time to get going. As Ted Berrigan's one-liner goes:

30
The fucking enemy shows up.

I should mention too that John Wieners earlier that year in Boston showed Frank a number of Charles Olson's poems, and that—together with much consideration of Ezra Pound's *Cantos* and Hart Crane and William Carlos Williams's *In the American Grain*, which came out that year, as did John Ashbery's *Some Trees* (chosen over Frank's manuscript, apparently somewhat grudgingly, by Auden for the Yale prize) and Proust—Olson seems to have gotten into O'Hara's poem, mostly in the way of format, or how the lines look on the page. I should mention a lot more—the cast of just literati on hand on the poem's elaborate mental movie set includes D.H. Lawrence, Aristotle, Samuel Beckett, Ovid, Rimbaud, Byron's *Manfred*, and "Negative Capability" à la Keats (so many of these absorbed years earlier—and here I am omitting the movies proper!)—but that will have to do.

Like a lot of Frank's poems, both long and short, "In Memory of My Feelings" is saturated with detail but in "In Memory" the saturation is intensified by being largely what the poem is about, the amplitude and multiplicity of person—or persons, as the poem is made of many shifts among persons and their circumstances—and, equally, of words—and of words committed to as nuanced, sensational fact. It is a pledge to circumstance versus any "dealable-with system," to a fluent and variable self rather than static continuity of same. Frank's term for this, inspired by reading Pound, was "simultaneity." If the poem has a hero, as it sometimes flirtatiously proclaims, that person is astir in his own and the world's simultaneities—all shifters and syntax, sometimes dangerously overboard: "A hit? *Ergo* swim." Like "Howl," it is a history poem with its own attitude towards one's own experience as the true locus of history. For all the detail, it is no less topographically spacious and airy, a real travelogue in scale. But the poem's saturation makes it a kind of echo chamber—every word counts, and so many words intermittently find their doubles or mirror images elsewhere down the page, along O'Hara's associative track—the relief being that as the poem echoes itself, it changes, which is very much the point. In perpetual metamorphosis, all forces, all names are aspects of one another. (Which may be why, as symbols go, the recombinant "serpent" of "In Memory of My Feelings" is an all-purpose one.)

A year after O'Hara wrote this poem, I entered college. At 18, a freshman, I showed up for my first class in an advanced undergraduate program intriguingly called Identification and Criticism of Ideas, a seminar about the nature of tragedy. Looking around the table at the students assembled for this first meeting, the professor, a drama critic named Gerald Weales, smiled broadly and said: "You may not know it, but you are all Existentialists." I mention this because "In Memory of My Feelings" is an Existentialist poem insofar as it proceeds from Jean-Paul Sartre, whose *Being and Nothingness* also appeared for the first time in English in 1956, and from much else in Western philosophy beside. In fact, it goes some way toward if not exactly solving, then *dissolving* Sartre's problem, the problem of anyone's substantive existence and the problem of how language and the observable world absurdly refuse to recognize one another. "They hadn't read *Being and Nothingness* for nothing," wrote Frank in a memoir later ("they" being the artists of his generation).

But Weales was right in this respect: that we were all, witless or not, as young students in 1957 existentialists, or he might have said all abstract-expressionists or Baby Beatniks or New American Poets, because that is where we were starting from, with such designations as baseline culture, something to proceed with, to bounce off of, and from which to enter.

As far as I know, O'Hara read "In Memory of My Feelings" in public only once, at a solo reading at the New School for Social Research, June

22, 1962. I introduced. Frank read smoothly and at speed. filmed in the courtyard of the school for broadcast as part of WNDT-TV educational television series that included other readings there that summer by Kenneth Koch, Marianne Moore, and Robert Lowell. Frank's reading was never aired. Later, when in 1964 I started co-producing some art programs for the same station, I asked about the program and was told that it had not been aired because O'Hara's voice was considered "too fruity for educational TV;" when I further inquired as to what had happened to the film itself, one director at the station said that any footage not broadcast after six months had probably been erased—the implication being that the document of O'Hara reading had suffered this fate. Of course, it's possible that the film still exists, tossed, maybe moldering in some crate at NET. It was the best reading I ever heard O'Hara give. During it, as it happened, I was sitting next to Kenneth Koch to the far left of the podium; when Frank finished reading "In Memory of My Feelings," Kenneth murmured, "Gee, it really is a great poem."

IN MEMORY OF MY FEELINGS
   to Grace Hartigan

1
My quietness has a man in it, he is transparent
and he carries me quietly, like a gondola, through the streets.
He has several likenesses, like stars and years, like numerals.

My quietness has a number of naked selves,
so many pistols I have borrowed to protect myselves
from creatures who too readily recognize my weapons
and have murder in their heart!
                  though in winter
they are warm as roses, in the desert
taste of chilled anisette.
             At times, withdrawn,
I rise into the cool skies
and gaze on at the imponderable world with the simple identification
of my colleagues, the mountains. Manfred climbs to my nape,
speaks, but I do not hear him,

I'm too blue.
An elephant takes up his trumpet,
money flutters from the windows of cries, silk stretching its mirror
across shoulder blades. A gun is "fired."
One of me rushes
to window #13 and one of me raises his whip and one of me
flutters up from the center of the track amidst the pink flamingoes,
and underneath their hooves as they round the last turn my lips
are scarred and brown, brushed by tails, masked in dirt's lust,
definition, open mouths gasping for the cries of the bettors for the
lungs of earth.
So many of my transparencies could not resist the race!
Terror in earth, dried mushrooms, pink feathers, tickets,
a flaking moon drifting across the muddied teeth,
the imperceptible moan of covered breathing,
love of the serpent!
I am underneath its leaves as the hunter crackles and pants
and bursts, as the barrage balloon drifts behind a cloud
and animal death whips out its flashlight,
whistling
and slipping the glove off the trigger hand. The serpent's eyes
redden at sight of those thorny fingernails, he is so smooth!
My transparent selves
flail about like vipers in a pail, writhing and hissing
without panic, with a certain justice of response
and presently the aquiline serpent comes to resemble the Medusa.

2
The dead hunting
and the alive, ahunted.
My father, my uncle,
my grand-uncle and the several aunts. My
grand-aunt dying for me, like a talisman, in the war,
before I had even gone to Borneo
her blood vessels rushed to the surface
and burst like rockets over the wrinkled
invasion of the Australians, her eyes aslant

like the invaded, but blue like mine.
An atmosphere of supreme lucidity,
                              humanism,
the mere existence of emphasis,
                              a rusted barge
painted orange against the sea
full of Marines reciting the Arabian ideas
which are a proof in themselves of seasickness
which is a proof in itself of being hunted.
A hit? *ergo* swim.
                    My 10   my 19,
my 9,   and the several years. My
12 years since they all died, philosophically speaking.
And now the coolness of a mind
like a shuttered suite in the Grand Hotel
where mail arrives for my incognito,
                              whose façade
has been slipping into the Grand Canal for centuries;
rockets splay over a *sposalizio*,
                         fleeing into night
from their Chinese memories, and it is a celebration
the trying desperately to count them as they die.
But who will stay to be these numbers
when all the lights are dead?

3
The most arid stretch is often richest,
the hand lifting towards a fig tree from hunger
                                   digging
and there is water, clear, supple, or there
deep in the sand where death sleeps, a murmurous bubbling
proclaims the blackness that will ease and burn.
You preferred the Arabs? but they didn't stay to count
their inventions, racing into sands, converting themselves into
so many,
          embracing, at Ramadan, the tenderest effigies of
themselves with penises shorn by the hundreds, like a camel

ravishing a goat.

        And the mountainous-minded Greeks could speak
of time as a river and step across it into Persia, leaving the pain
at home to be converted into statuary. I adore the Roman copies.
And the stench of the camel's spit I swallow,
and the stench of the whole goat. For we have advanced, France,
together into a new land, like the Greeks, where one feels nostalgic
for mere ideas, where truth lies on its deathbed like an uncle
and one of me has a sentimental longing for number,
as has another for the ball gowns of the Directoire and yet
another for "Destiny, Paris, destiny!"

            or "Only a king may kill a king."

How many selves are there in a war hero asleep in names? under
a blanket of platoon and fleet, orderly. For every seaman
with one eye closed in fear and twitching arm at a sigh for Lord Nelson,
he is all dead; and now a meek subaltern writhes in his bedclothes
with the fury of a thousand, violating an insane mistress
who has only herself to offer his multitudes.

        Rising,
he wraps himself in the burnoose of memories against the heat of life
And over the sands he goes to take an algebraic position *in re*
A sun of fear shining not too bravely. He will ask himselves to
vote on fear before he feels a tremor,

        as runners arrive from the mountains
bearing snow, proof that the mind's obsolescence is still capable
of intimacy. His mistress will follow him across the desert
like a goat, towards a mirage which is something familiar about
one of his innumerable wrists,

        and lying in an oasis one day,
playing catch with coconuts, they suddenly smell oil.

4
Beneath these lives
the ardent lover of history hides,

        tongue out
leaving a globe of spit on a taut spear of grass

and leaves off rattling his tail a moment
to admire this flag.
                    I'm looking for my Shanghai Lil.
Five years ago, enamored of fire-escapes, I went to Chicago,
an eventful trip: the fountains! the Art institute, the Y
for both sexes, absent Christianity.
                              At 7, before Jane
was up, the copper lake stirred against the sides
of a Norwegian freighter; on the deck a few dirty men,
tired of night, watched themselves in the water
as years before the German prisoners on the *Prinz Eugen*
dappled the Pacific with their sores, painted purple
by a Naval doctor.
                        Beards growing, and the constant anxiety
over looks. I'll shave before she wakes up. Sam Goldwyn
spent $2,000,000 on Anna Sten, but Grushenka left America.
One of me is standing in the waves, an ocean bather,
or I am naked with a plate of devils at my hip.
                                              Grace
to be born and live as variously as possible. The conception
of the masque barely suggests the sordid identifications.
I am a Hittite in love with a horse. I don't know what blood's
in me I feel like an African prince I am a girl walking downstairs
in a red pleated dress with heels I am a champion taking a fall
I am a jockey with a sprained ass-hole I am the light mist
                              in which a face appears
and it is another face of blonde I am a baboon eating a banana
I am a dictator looking at his wife I am a doctor eating a child
and the child's mother smiling I am a Chinaman climbing a mountain
I am a child smelling his father's underwear I am an Indian
sleeping on a scalp
                    and my pony is stamping in the birches,
and I've just caught sight of the *Niña,* the *Pinta* and the *Santa Maria.*
            What land is this, so free?
                              I watch
the sea at the back of my eyes, near the spot where I think
in solitude as pine trees groan and support the enormous winds,

they are humming *L'Oiseau de feu!*
They look like gods, these whitemen,
and they are bringing me the horse I fell in love with on the frieze.

5
And now it is the serpent's turn.
I am not quite you, but almost, the opposite of visionary.
You are coiled around the central figure,
the heart
that bubbles with red ghosts, since to move is to love
and the scrutiny of all things is syllogistic,
the startled eyes of the dikdik, the bush full of white flags
fleeing a hunter,
which is our democracy
but the prey
is always fragile and like something, as a seashell can be
a great Courbet, if it wishes. To bend the ear of the outer world.

When you turn your head
can you feel your heels, undulating? that's what it is
to be a serpent. I haven't told you of the most beautiful things
in my lives, and watching the ripple of their loss disappear
along the shore, underneath ferns,
face downward in the ferns
my body, the naked host to my many selves, shot
by a guerrilla warrior or dumped from a car into ferns
which are themselves *journalières.*
The hero, trying to unhitch his parachute,
stumbles over me. It is our last embrace.
And yet
I have forgotten my loves, and chiefly that one, the cancerous
statue which my body could no longer contain,
against my will
against my love
become art,
I could not change it into history
and so remember it,

and I have lost what is always and everywhere
present, the scene of my selves, the occasion of these ruses,
which I myself and singly must now kill

                          and save the serpent in their midst.

The next poem, and the last for tonight, immediately follows "In Memory of My Feelings" in the *Collected*, and is the first of Frank's "I do this I do that" poems, or at least certainly the first with what soon became the convention of taking a walk in the New York streets, "A Step Away from Them." Specifically, the timing of the occasion for "A Step Away" is plain, August 16, 1956, and among the happenstances—blotting out the rest (though the rest share similar deadly intimations) and forcing a removal of person in the instant, the going "on"—is the registering of the early deaths, in quick succession, of three mythological figures: Bunny Lang at 32 on July 29, John Latouche at 38 on August 7, and Jackson Pollock, aged 44, on August 11th.

A STEP AWAY FROM THEM

It's my lunch hour, so I go
for a walk among the hum-colored
cabs. First, down the sidewalk
where laborers feed their dirty
glistening torsos sandwiches
and Coca-Cola, with yellow helmets
on. They protect them from falling
bricks, I guess. Then onto the
avenue where skirts are flipping
above heels and blow up over
grates. The sun is hot, but the
cabs stir up the air. I look
at bargains in wristwatches. There
are cats playing in sawdust.
                          On
to Times Square, where the sign
blows smokes over my head, and higher
the waterfall pours lightly. A

Negro stands in a doorway with a
toothpick, languorously agitating.
A blonde chorus girl clicks: he
smiles and rubs his chin. Everything
suddenly honks: it is 12:40 of
a Thursday.
               Neon in daylight is a
great pleasure, as Edwin Denby would
write, as are light bulbs in daylight.
I stop for a cheeseburger at JULIET'S
CORNER. Guilietta Masina, wife of
Federico Fellini, *é bell' atrice.*
And chocolate malted. A lady in
foxes on such a day puts her poodle
in a cab.
               There are several Puerto
Ricans on the avenue today, which
makes it beautiful and warm. First
Bunny died, then John Latouche,
then Jackson Pollock. But is the
earth as full as life was full, of them?
And one has eaten and one walks,
past the magazines with nudes
and the posters for BULLFIGHT and
the Manhattan Storage Warehouse,
which they'll soon tear down. I
used to think they had the Armory
Show there.
               A glass of papaya juice
and back to work. My heart is in my
pocket, it is Poems by Pierre Reverdy.

So there. There is always some death in an "I do this I do that" poem. And, as in Emily Dickinson, *After great pain a formal feeling comes.* The formality that binds the elements together is Frank's classy diction, "languorously agitating." It's this poem that makes the two previous ones retroactively, in some ways terribly, prophetic. *What is happen-*

ing to me, allowing for lies and exaggerations which I try to avoid, goes into my poems—and thus what presumably happened when it did goes as writing into the present tense, and so precisely "goes" the specific, if rather fitful incidental "now" of the poem that one wonders, the mystery deepens: when is the poem, the energetic fact of which we have before us, actually written? Nothing of the poem goes away, and part of its function, O'Hara tells us, is to be restorative of life's detail, of which the writing is a part, as well. It will be just what it is and just what happens. The feeling is the poem is written as one reads it, which all of a sudden seems perfectly normal.

The sequence ends there, and rolls on into the Odes, Lunch Poems, Love Poems (Tentative Title) and so on. Taking a walk turns out to be a design for existence—anyone's particular "walk in life," so to speak—the clearest evidence for which is the stepping along, the breathing in and out, for which the verbal montage—shot and cut—is analogous: out is looking, in is thought (Frank's exhales generally seem longer than his intakes). Up, metaphysical in previous poems, now seems merely a vector for the camera eye to travel along, panning, from street level. Stir up the air. There are no falling bricks, no more pronoun struggles, but a classical sureness of declension, how each arrives by turn in appropriate space. There's a catch in the throat, a snap, at the turn, where an absence is felt. The lines, all detail (chin) and coordinate (higher) enriched by qualification (beautiful and warm), are stacked like girders, the whole condensation like ice, pulsating.

In "My Heart" O'Hara had written, "You can't plan on the heart, but / the better part of it, my poetry, is open." And later (though, having put it differently in the next sentence, he went back and crossed it out): "Poetry is life to me." Reverdy is what comes to hand, coterminous with the poem Frank O'Hara writes in its moment, but it's pertinent that when, July 8, 1822, one month short of his thirtieth birthday, Percy Shelley's body washed up on the beach, Poems by John Keats, in his friend Leigh Hunt's copy, was found in his jacket pocket.

Poets House, 2006

I like to play a game with my conceptual artist friends, for whom art is more or less strictly an idea-driven affair. David (David Ireland is one), I say, make me a list of all the ideas in the world. The point being, there can't be many of them, or not many really are worth considering. Just as in poetry Ezra Pound once remarked that there are only six or seven emotions available to write about, and every time I think of this I can't remember which ones Ezra listed. Did what Agnes Martin later called "abstract emotion"—waking up happy or sad for no discernible reason—make the cut? Anyhow, in the frame of devising a lecture, the opposite proves true: all of a sudden there are too many ideas. Thinking ahead to this occasion, after the initial surprise delight of being designated the speaker of choice, I found myself several months in advance with enough notes for three or more such talks. What to do? We'll be here all night.

Well, it's an educational setting. The fabulously art-happy painter and teacher Hans Hofmann, the one time I met him, stood in his Provincetown studio surrounded by five or six big paintings each markedly distinct in manner from all the others. Casting his eye from one to the next, he threw up his hands in probably mock-despair: "Ach, I have too many styles!" he said. In those days, style was the outward manifestation of whatever idea hung in the air. ("I see you have your own ideas," said Gorky a little nervously when he first entered de Kooning's studio in the 1930s.) Hofmann probably had more good ideas when he was teaching than when he quit and went on to make what stand as his best, most impulsive pictures. What seems most amazing about Hofmann the teacher is how varied and un-Hofmannlike the work of so many of his students became. He himself had very definite ideas of what art should be, but his students were people like Allan Kaprow, George Segal, Larry Rivers, Jane Freilicher, Red Grooms and others who would not become abstract painters—or painters at all, some of them—in anything like the Hofmann mold. Among Hofmann's visitors that afternoon in Provincetown was Larry Rivers, who, shortly after we exited Hofmann's studio, all of us sitting on the deck outside, began talking about his difficulties as a father (he was having trouble communicating with one of his sons); whereupon Hofmann suddenly said to Larry, "You have no talent for growing old"—which was, it turned out, once it was reiterated, OK for Hofmann to say, but what Larry had heard his old teacher say was "You have no talent"—flat out, period—at which Larry was understandably chagrined.

It seems that talent is something you hear about in school. Poetry and art-school teachers sometimes act like talent scouts. And schooling is partly what I am talking about tonight—along with expectations (great and not), what is expected of poetry and art, and, ultimately perhaps, some sense of happiness or the promise of happiness in the fact of being an artist. My first best teacher in poetry was Kenneth Koch. In his poetry workshop at the New School for Social Research in New York, which I entered in 1959, and in his poetry, Kenneth was a tireless improviser; the dazzle in the classroom involved watching him think out loud, in front of you; he consistently invented fresh analogies for the pleasures he took in the poetry he admired, and hitting on those, registering the extra pleasure of arriving at unexpected edges in his own thought, Kenneth flashed his wide, bright Kenneth smile and laughed, ha-ha, right on the beat. He didn't stop to congratulate himself, the world he found he could envision so eloquently was just that great, even greater for being articulated in return. "I think you are very talented," he wrote in pencil on one of the manuscripts I submitted after the first class session. I thought "talented" meant something like accomplished. Later I understood that what Kenneth meant was that talent was strictly for openers, a professional responsibility to take charge of, to cultivate and grow. A significant quote in class from Paul Valéry stays apropos: "A poem is written by someone other than the poet and addressed to someone other than the reader."

Kenneth was, and continues to be, central to my education. His conception of poetry as a form of nearly materialized, physical excitement made me see not just poetry but the world in and outside poetry differently. Not only did he encourage me in my writing but without proselytizing he revealed how being a poet could be a sensible pursuit—sensible in every respect—for a grown person. More about that later. Now I want to read a poem of Kenneth's that really is the thing I've had most in mind since it appeared in print not along after he died four years ago this month:

PARADISO

There is no way not to be excited
When what you have been disillusioned by raises its head
From its arms and seems to want to talk to you again.
You forget home and family
And set off on foot or in your automobile
And go to where you believe this form of reality
May dwell. Not finding it there, you refuse
Any further contact
Until you are back again trying to forget
The only thing that moved you (it seems) and gave what you
        forever will have
But in the form of a disillusion.
Yet often, looking toward the horizon
There—inimical to you?—is that something you have never found
And that, without those who came before you, you could never
        have imagined.
How could you have thought there was one person who could
        make you
Happy and that happiness was not the uneven
Phenomenon you have known it to be? Why do you keep believing
        in this
Reality so dependent on the time allowed it
That it has less to do with your exile from the age you are
Than from everything else life promised that you could do?

The poem is twenty lines of radically varied lengths, with an unfolding argument that makes it feel like an extended sonnet.

Why the poem is called "Paradiso" no one I've discussed it with claims to know for sure, though rereading Dante provides some surefire clues. The language Kenneth employs is Dante-esque in its compression and clarity, especially the first image:

> When what you have been disillusioned by raises its head
> From its arms and seems to want to talk to you again—

which is also the only image, one that stirs the poem into action. There has been an impasse in the scenario, and the poem starts out as a resumption of possibility—of life's, or love's, promise. Like Dante, too, is the feeling of overriding mystery and a kind of questioning that serves only, as do Dante's questions to Beatrice in Paradise, to deepen the mystery.

But Kenneth's language in this poem is also Freudian—I mean, in the style of Sigmund Freud, who as an idea man may have been more dependent on his extraordinarily inventive prose style than his followers have acknowledged. The poem, almost certainly finished not long before Kenneth died—apparently, he had begun it twenty years earlier, in Paris—is about happiness, something that Freud spent a great deal of time writing about, largely because, like anyone, he saw so little of it around or in him and yet so much evidence that happiness was what people were after in their everyday behavior whether they were conscious of it or not. (Here I should probably add that Kenneth himself spent many years in Freudian psychoanalysis, which, for one thing, relieved him of a stammer that was very pronounced when I first met him.)

"Paradiso" is about happiness, the promise of happiness, its illusionary, hence disappointing aspect, and in a certain way, its relentlessness, here presented as not abstract at all. "What is characteristic of illusions is that they are derived from human wishes," wrote Freud. Stendhal identified Beauty as nothing other than the promise of happiness. Hope of Heaven, of some ultimate bliss, perhaps enters, too. "Paradiso" is a very unusual poem in the Koch repertory. Kenneth is famous as a comic poet, many or most of his poems are predominantly funny—when he was young, on the basis of both his poems and his behavior, ever the cut-up, his best friends John Ashbery and Frank O'Hara dubbed him "Dr. Fun." But "Paradiso," odd as it may be, is not a funny poem; only one poem in Kenneth's work compares to it in consistency of feeling, and that one is called, appropriately enough, "Fate." The earlier of the two, "Fate" addresses a bygone youth of intense affections and expectations, "the time plowing forward," as he feels it, even then; in "Paradiso," with time now at a premium, we overhear the poet conversing, somewhat deliriously to be sure, with his soul.

One of the pleasures of Kenneth's poetry occurs in his taking a calm, reasonable tone—embodying reason or logic itself—to extremes; it becomes sublime, just a fraction of an inch short of, or beyond, the ridiculous, so that, getting there with Kenneth, you laugh knowingly, yet wholeheartedly, with the event. In "Paradiso," which I take to be at once totally baffling and perfectly true, both calm and reason, though present, are subject to fits: the syntax commences plainly, veers off, regathers its nonetheless ever-twisty, kaleidoscopic logic, and lands forcefully on two tough, crystallizing questions, the first quite normal and the last utterly (triumphantly?) enigmatic:

> How could you have thought there was one person who could
> make you
> Happy and that happiness was not the uneven
> Phenomenon you have known it to be? Why do you keep believing
> in this
> Reality so dependent on the time allowed it
> That it has less to do with your exile from the age you are
> Than from everything else life promised that you could do?

There is no way not to be excited . . . Excitement, the happiness in being excited, in being possessed of a vivid sensibility, and of communicating this in poetry—largely, this was Kenneth's message. His commitment to it had nothing arcane in its thoroughness, and no guarantees. His being gleeful on purpose is like Keats's "deliberate happiness" (which troubled Yeats in that it didn't jibe with the sadness of Keats's life as it unfolded—Yeats didn't get it). This purposefulness—and Kenneth's characteristic head-up, spine-straight yet marvelously limber posture that went with it—seemed practical, practicable. I found it palpable too in the red-penciled sheets of Kenneth's poetry stuffed into black spring blinders seeing them later in his living room as Janice tossed her *bon mots* from the kitchen, stirring chicken in the pot, and young, intense Katherine sat quietly on the sofa—a life ordinary enough but for that determination to infuse or join with it, so to speak, to make one's day. Taken together, these things let me see how poetry could be a way to lead one's life, an occupation in the world, no more special, if no less absurd, than any other, but available to me as nothing else with anything of like interest at the time.

So Kenneth's lessons during that spring I was his student continued after class as we walked down 12th Street away from the New School and, in his soft voice and perfectly formed and evenly punctuated sentences, he began delivering breathy, variously lyric or hilarious commentaries on signs in shop windows, shapes of clouds, an overheard remark followed by his rendition of it in lines of blank verse or a 32-bar blues parody, and yet another flurry of wit in response to whatever I might however stumblingly venture in-between. And:

   Sky
woof woof!
  harp.

Sky, said Frank O'Hara, between buildings—this was in 1956, three or four years before I knew either of them—and *woof woof!* went undercutting, substantiating Kenneth. Then *harp*, exhaled Frank arriving at the curb as the light changed. Later indoors, one of them, Kenneth probably, types it up, and they give to John Myers who has asked for new work for his Tibor de Nagy Gallery magazine *Semicolon*.

   Sky
woof woof!
  harp

Sky
woof woof!
harp.

Same three lines repeated twelve times down the page.

Was Kenneth happy? The question is grossly beside the point. When
he was at a low point, being treated in Texas for what would prove to be
fatal leukemia, to keep his spirit up friends sent him poems, little hand-
made books of them, drawings, postcards, whatever came to hand, all
with Kenneth in mind. Poetry made him happy. His habitual doubts
and suspicions abated; he understood that his friends loved him dearly,
and this made him easier to love, as well. "Poetry," said Kenneth in a
final interview, "temporarily improves the human situation." The same
can be said for happiness. Happiness—"the least and best of human
attainments," Frank called it—generally goes only so far, like enlight-
enment, like artistic success.

As that spring went along, Kenneth also became the one who clued me
to the incidental connections between poetry and art. He would flesh
out his description of what was happening in a John Ashbery poem by
telling how a painting by Jane Freilicher projected the sensation of big
pink flowers in sunlight on a city windowsill so strongly that you had
an inkling of what it might be to sit there so effulgent, a sentient flower.
That spring I saw, among many things in quick succession, my first de
Koonings, the sizzling "landscape abstractions," and in a group show,
Rauschenberg's stupendous Angora-goat assemblage, *Monogram*. The
newness and variety and appropriateness, levity and seriousness all
at once of hometown New York art kept stopping me in my tracks. I
understood little but was inspired to see how, typical of the city, so
many contrary types of energy collided and fit.

Because the art world then was small, the interrelations Kenneth spoke
of were easy to see and you could assume how, behind and in front of
the works themselves, the poets, painters, musicians and theater people
and dancers, the critics who tagged along, and the intellectual audience
altogether, were talking together, which made the idea of being an

artist a fluent thing, which you can't assume today. At this point in our culture, it seems necessary to say that the art world isn't art. The art world is a formidable albeit relatively small-time institution or set of them that at best facilitates the practice and general enjoyment of visual art. Unless you are so disposed or can't do otherwise, you don't commit to an institution as if that it is where you mean to live. With the art world comes art-world art. Art itself does not create this situation. Art-world (or museum-type) art is the certifiable art of galleries, fairs, biennials, museums, art magazines, know-it-all collectors and big bad critics. There really is no complaining about the art world. You are either in it or out, and if in and severely discontented, you should leave. To inhabit it, you had better be prepared. Despite the rumors, it is not a conspiracy; it is more like Jean Cocteau's Infernal Machine. It is all as Byzantine as Russia.

Poetry has no such world. In its place, one sometimes hears the word "community," which in common usage weighs in as either a wishful metonym for ghetto (the squeal of a wounded animal somewhere the far side of town) or a rallying cry for collective leverage. "The International Community," for its part, as wielded by businessmen and politicians, carries bare-knuckle coercive overtones—another incarnation of the Big Stick. The visual artist who speaks of "community" generally tries to take the self-important art world down a peg, by asserting her or his relevance as "artist citizen." Happily, albeit in highly specific, usually carefully protected, contexts, this works. For poets, the word "community" signals merely the wish to be not entirely isolated. One used to say "the scene." "The poetry community" indicates nothing more than that x-number of poets know one another and/or one another's poems and another, vaguely larger number know the names of more poets and a lot less about their poems. Strangely, despite the Internet, there is less international connectedness now than there was in the mid-twentieth century. (Despite globalization, one is less likely to know now what the poets in Ghana are doing, or have done, than in 1959.) "What do the poets do?" a neighbor kept asking in Bolinas when suddenly, during the '70s, a lot of poets had moved to that sublimely welcoming California coastal village. Finally, she told me she had figured out what the poets do: "They laugh a lot and say funny things to each other."

Poetry, one concludes, has a space, the space of a page, a room in which it can be read and, with luck, enjoyed.

Can one usefully compare the world of art and this putative other world of poetry? Momentously, in the 1980s, I read in the *Village Voice* of a poll of women in New York designed to find out what sort of men, if any, they liked to be with. They said poets were very low on the scale—even, as one woman said, "if they rhyme." However, artists rated very high; they were typified as "sensitive, soulful, and they draw your portrait on a napkin." A little later, also in the *Voice*, I read Peter Schjeldahl—until then described, as I am still, in art-magazine contributors notes, as "a poet who also writes about art"—declaring that being a poet no longer interested him because poetry lacked the requisite cultural currency that visual art ostensibly had going for it. Fantastic, I thought—bypassing initial rage and dismay—and how indeed is this currency measured? A colleague of mine in the art history program at the Art Institute plans a session at next year's College Art Association with the topic heading "Are Today's MFAs the MBAs of Tomorrow?" No poet can lay claim to any comparable administrative function. But why not? There is no reason not to be in business if there is some business to be done. Poets look askance at the art world economy, its boosterism, feeding frenzies and attendance figures, its amusing orthodoxy of developmental volatility, favoring whatever graduates to be the next museumable thing. But then few nowadays believe that poetry is regular work or that it has a serious history. Years ago, a cherished painter friend snapped at me in what I now think must have been a rare moment of spite: "Maybe poetry is a residue—I've worked my ass off for thirty years." True, poets themselves don't tally what they do as day labor, though sometimes they may wish there were a commensurate invoicing system for it. Poetry, being, as Frank O'Hara said, "less immediately apprehensible," has its durable density, its fructifying nonsense, its interventions as subtle, as surreptitious as a leech field, its ingredients percolating through the common culture as we speak.

We live in an unstable culture. This is an old story by now and has gotten to be practically the only story we know. Whatever more entertaining communal scenario was once available now appears recondite.

If poetry and art have any assignment it is to make up the universe each time from scratch, hoping to uncover some plausibly declarative thread with enough connective tissue and shine to put it across. As a job description—or even as a condition of freedom to be celebrated—this implies a lot of uncompensated overtime. What Thomas Crow has called "the era of freely conceived art," begun in eighteenth-century Paris, keeps us supplied with scandalous surpluses of art and poetry that nobody asked for and for which no concordance is given. (Arguably, for example, all of High Modernism's plausible meanings were worked out, if not by ESP, then by ingenious modes of subliminal pattern recognition.) "We poets know nothing," sang ancient Hesiod, "only what the muses tell us." Modernity's default muses have been private sensibility, abstract forms, and a general culture made manifest as what we now call "media."

William Carlos Williams once wrote something to the effect that a poem should aim to constitute an event—"a revelation" is what he said—in the language in which it is written. In a way, that seems little enough to ask. In art and poetry, you think at least something ought to happen: *show* or *tell me* is, so to speak, the viewer/reader's share. A poet may or may not believe his senses, but he knows that whatever accumulation he has of words in his given language is one sense among others. Visuality's demonstrative advantage is its swiftness of delivery, its all-at-once-ness; you get the image in a flash, "faster than thought," as Edwin Denby remarked. How an image works in memory is mysterious—you don't memorize pictures the way poetry can be memorized, by rote. A poem and a picture both work at the skin of consciousness. The specific power of contemporary poetry may lie in its arcane randomness, while art in the galleries and museums tends to have a canonical look. A poet's collected work over time will be usually about many different things, possessed of diverse effects, and often done in different styles, even though the characteristic tone may be consistent. Poets, I think, have a stronger and more richly phantasmagoric sense of audience than visual artists who nowadays conceive almost exclusively of people in the business (other artists, dealers, patrons, curators, assorted gargoyles) staring at their work—staring it down, I mean. The air of art is poisoned with criticism. That may be why visual art is too often one-note—the same basic imagery, the same emotion or idea repeated and standardized—except when it isn't. (There are, as ever, major exceptions.)

Simply put, words traditionally work deeper, longer than sign language, than images, but images can be faster and, for now, more memorable. Economically, poetry's advantage is that words are free and paper recyclable, whereas tube colors and video monitors are expensive and high-maintenance and shipping and handling and insurance and, glory notwithstanding, the design and construction of major-statement art museums, even more so, through the roof. The downside is, good poetry tends to be highly nuanced and nuance is not much tolerated in the time famine that is today. Further, there is no printed poetry criticism of any value at all; reviewers and presenters in their introductions discuss the character of the poet, not the poems, and cloistered scholars tend to miss the contexts of ordinariness and wonder where poems have their impetus. As a result, few people know of, or know how to read, the lively poetry that is being written. I don't exactly stay awake nights wondering how the art world—not to mention, how America as a whole—could benefit from reading more great poetry. But the deficit is plain. The art magazines and catalogues are full of evidence that the literature artists and critics read is mostly middlebrow (an old term, admittedly, but newly applicable), including officially sanctioned melodramas in prose and verse and hurry-up translations of the latest European thinkers.

Expository writing with a speculative philosophical bent, which is what most so-called "theory" is, tends to be stylistically intricate and wild enough in the (mostly French, though sometimes Italian or Polish) original as to require the most inspired and knowledgeable translator to bring it across. This is rarely managed, so in English the writing is unduly opaque and art students who are assigned substantial readings in it get lengthy explanations which usually reduce the matter to a few memorable keywords—"deconstruction," "the Other," "late Capitalism"—that don't mean anything. This is somewhat the same way poetry and other imaginative literature is conveyed, if at all, in school. It wards off all pleasure of the text, and so, arguably, it is the best argument for reading poetry for yourself, alone in a corner. American poetry is more scattered in its understandings of what poetry is or can be than the art world is about art. That is because understanding poetry is dominated by agenda either sentimentalist or professorial or both while the art world is, if nothing else, more worldly and urbane (and at this juncture, poetry could use—as a pressure gauge, at least—a little of the art world's sense of seasonal fashions).

A truly sad factor, long endemic to the art world but new and, given the stakes, particularly egregious among poets presently is a sort of grabby hyper-professionalism: After John Ashbery's reading to a full house in an elegant library space at the University of California at Berkeley a few years ago I overheard two students in the graduate writing program exchanging impressions of what were to them the no-doubt palpable shortcomings in Ashbery's verses: "I'm going to blow that guy out of the water!" said student A to student B, triumphantly. I walked on, stunned by the young master's assertion of such a feral sense of his own promise. What did I expect? What voice of reasonable tolerance or long-practiced cynicism rushed in to tell me that as distasteful as it may be, such is after all literally a world-class attitude? The hard lesson, learned repeatedly over time, is that the world in all its classy nastiness is with us no matter the apparent niceties of the setting; high-minded as art would hope to be, it offers no exemption. (For art students, failure to get this message and get it quick can mean from four years to a lifetime of debilitating resentment). The "anxiety of influence" is something we all get used to; for Jackson Pollock, as the scholars never fail to remind us, Picasso was "the guy to beat." ("Getting in the ring with Tolstoy" was the literary brawler's conception of the same raw deal.) But that brash colloquy in the stacks at Berkeley was something else. Freud wrote of happiness as "the belated fulfillment of a prehistoric wish. For this reason wealth brings so little happiness. Money was not a childhood wish." Nor, for that matter, was fame; approval is another matter, or a sense that what one does in the world is *in* the world one wishes to exist in. All of Dante's poetry reads as a perpetual induction ceremony to such a world—or, as he says, the "company" he would hope to share it with. In the meadow of Limbo, on the outskirts of Hell, "on the enameled green," Dante sees Virgil join anew with the four great shades of classic poets, so that altogether they make a circle of five:

Thus I saw assembled the fair school of that lord of highest song who, like an eagle, soars above the rest. After they had talked awhile together, they turned to me with sign of salutation, at which my master smiled; and far more honor still they showed me, for they made me one of their company, so that I was sixth amid so much wisdom. Thus we went onward to the light, talking of things it is well to pass in silence, even as it was well to speak of them there.

In Dante's number scheme, six leaves room for a seventh, or 7-8-9 (three more), or multiples thereof. This is good news. Dante is not being preemptive. In the *Convivio*, he announces his ambition to achieve a certain level of nobility in his work, "not that I am a good worker, but that I aspire after such." There, too, is the beautiful sense of destiny—not predestination as such, but that somehow one is led by long practice to an accumulation that is one's art—just that: that it may add up. So Rudy Burckhardt related one story of de Kooning confessing that, even as a young painter, when he went through the subway turnstile he always expected to hear the bell ring a little louder for him; and another of how de Kooning told him: "What you do when you paint, you take a brush full of paint, get paint on the picture, and you have *fate*" (that is "faith," in Dutch accent).

Likewise, something said many years ago by Jasper Johns in an interview retains a fresh kind of nagging pertinence: "Art is either a complaint or appeasement," Johns told the poet David Shapiro. Perhaps not so surprising coming from such a contemplative artist as Johns, the sentence implies a form of supplication, expressive of his or someone's idea of a good time, a clear desire, tied to appetite, or what makes one want to live, beyond the sheer, inert organic fact of subsisting. As in Kenneth's poem, the excitement of a promise is adjunct to happiness, or a sign of it, like of an impending shower, which—*looking toward the horizon/There*—may be just a mirage.

Whatever it is, one has arrived, as Fate would have it, at whatever it is. Virgil Thomson, a marvelous composer and great no-nonsense critic, liked to say that there are three important things in life: work, friendship and passionate love; you can have two, Virgil said, but nobody gets all three. Kenneth heard Virgil say this, and so did I, and, because Virgil was given to repeating himself, we heard it on different occasions, widely spaced. I regret that Kenneth and I never collaborated on poems the way he and Frank did, but as it happens, we each wrote a poem responding to what Virgil said. Kenneth, seemingly taking Virgil's side, wrote:

YOU WANT A SOCIAL LIFE WITH FRIENDS

You want a social life, with friends,
A passionate love life and as well
To work hard every day. What's true
Is of these three you may have two
And two can pay you dividends
But never may have three.

There isn't time enough, my friends—
Though dawn begins, yet midnight ends—
To find the time to have love, work, and friends.
Michelangelo had feeling
For Vittoria and the Ceiling
But did he go to parties at day's end?

Homer nightly went to banquets
Wrote all day but had no lockets
Bright with pictures of his Girl.
I know one who loves and parties
And has done so since his thirties
But writes hardly anything at all.

My poem runs counter to Kenneth's and is resistant to Virgil's cautionary rule. The title of mine, incidentally, puts us in an imaginary picture by Chardin or Vermeer:

I chose love and friendship over
　　work, then
　　　　work and friendship over
　　suspended disbelief
　　　　　　　　— won't love conquer all?
　　　I'll never work again.
　　Don't call me.

Plowing onward, I may think less in terms of choices I might make
than of what is given, call it fate or destiny or simply what next comes to
hand. My desk seems permanently littered with evidence of the perennial unfinished; I treat the bulging folders and stray sheets like clients
in a dentist's waiting room, "Next!" and grab what surfaces. One day a
member of the Detroit Pistons says on TV, "Well, life can't be all peaches
and gravy," and within twenty-four hours Condoleezza Rice repeats
this malapropism word for word. Some life, you think—why live it? A
couple of years ago, at what doctors told me would be "end stage" of a
rather gruesome disease, I was confronted accordingly for the first time
with a life-or-death-determining choice. I remembered Achilles' reply
when asked what he missed most as he stomped around in the Land
of the Dead: *to be alive and see the light of the sun.* No bigger idea than
that seemed required to keep me going. Daylight, an appreciable *raison
d'être.* This past April in Kyoto, on a suitably overcast day in the rock
garden, I saw how every detail in the arrangement sat somehow identi-
cal to itself and distinct to each person strolling along the perimeter,
mind and matter intersecting in throbbing intermittence. There was
no big idea—just rocks and sand (or gravel) and whatever you took to
be the whole situation besides. You don't have to be a Buddhist to get
that; in fact, *that* is about where Buddhism or any -ism, any big idea,
ceases to be of interest. The living, breathing moment counts, in the
light of obvious fact.

Fairfield Porter liked to say, Light brings us the news of the universe.
The light here in Maine is famous—made so famously by painters:
Porter, Winslow Homer, Fitz Henry Lane, John Marin, Hartley, Avery,

Rudy Burckhardt, Yvonne Jacquette, Alex Katz, to name some. Porter's light now seems solidified, hanging in there, like a mood. The light in Alex Katz's landscape pictures is fabulously swift, but recently also soulful, commemorative: it is beautifully there in the picture and already gone in your mind when you think of it: a breath and a catastrophe in one glance.

> I thought of Chatterton, the marvelous boy,
> The sleepless soul that perished in his pride;
> Of him who walked in glory and in joy
> Following his plough, along the mountain side:
> By our own spirits are we deified:
> We poets in our youth begin in gladness;
> But thereof come in the end despondency and madness.

As a famous and all too normative version of artistic progress, Wordsworth's closing couplet is about as provocative and reliable a homily as Virgil Thomson's witticism about priorities. After all, Chatterton hardly gave himself a chance, committing suicide at 17, and Wordsworth was 45-going-on-80 when he wrote the poem, "Resolution and Independence," in 1815. By now you see how my experience has run distinctly counter to what Wordsworth proposed as an eternal verity, and how that is a leitmotif of this talk. One instance fresh in mind is the last reading that Robert Creeley gave in San Francisco, six years ago almost, and five before he died. Because by then he was severely prone to shortness of breath, Bob sat on stage to read his new poems, expansive as they were, in rhythms and rhymes that recalled anthology pieces of his youth out of Alfred Noyes, "Thanotopsis" and the like. (Though the actual push in them, reflective of the urgency Bob felt of old age and death, was gleaned from late Whitman.) There was a fresh, gleeful vigor delivered with Bob's typical outlaw dash. But the doggerel bent of some of the poems nonplussed a significant portion of the audience. Two rows ahead of me, a somewhat older contemporary of Bob's sternly shook his head. During the Q&A, what appeared to be an able student asked how Creeley, obviously an avant-garde master, could write such backward stuff, to which Bob replied, smiling and raising one arm in glad salute, "Because I can!"

I wrote this lecture with both Kenneth and Bob in mind, both of them now being demonstrably, frustratingly, out of reach. They were in some ways contradictory spirits, although I think as time went by their contradictions became so resolved as to be complementary in the fabric of the poetic company they both enjoyed. Artists you know as friends and heroes and teachers die, you miss their company, and what compensation there is, large enough to matter, arrives in the form of a wider, deeper—larger than life, one would almost venture to say—sense of their work, what it amounts to, where they took it, and how increasingly distinct as well as necessary it feels to be. In some cases, the work will seem less "the uneven phenomenon" it was while the person was still alive—you discover some aspect of it, an unexpected poem perhaps, that shows all the others in a new light. A fictional instance of this is in Pasternak's *Doctor Zhivago* where Zhivago's childhood friends gather, astonished and moved to read his posthumous poems; a real-life one was when Kenneth and I and others first went through the manuscripts Frank O'Hara had left more or less casually behind in his desk—like Keats' "new planet" swimming into our collective firmament. Did Kenneth have something up his sleeve when he left us "Paradiso"? Certainly, he had something significant about his whole life in mind. In the same book as "Paradiso" is another poem called "Proverb"—also unusual, this time about mortality and how swiftly it accomplishes its work:

> We living stand at the gate
> And life goes on.

Paul Mellon Lecture
Skowhegan School of Painting and Sculpture, 2006

Sudden Address was typeset in Martin Majoor's Scala and designed by
Kyle Schlesinger at the Cuneiform Press in January, 2007.
Second printing: September, 2010.